Get Them to
See It Your Way,
Right Away

Get Them to See It Your Way, Right Away

How to Persuade Anyone of Anything

Ruth Sherman

McGraw-Hill
New York   Chicago   San Francisco   Lisbon   London
Madrid   Mexico City   Milan   New Delhi
San Juan   Seoul   Singapore   Sydney   Toronto

2 3 4 5 6 7 8 9 0 DOC/DOC 0 9 8 7 6 5 4

ISBN 0-07-142273-0

Library of Congress Cataloging-in-Publication Data

Sherman, Ruth.
    Get them to see it your way, right away : how to persuade anyone of anything / by Ruth Sherman.— 1st ed.
        p.   cm.
    Includes index.
    ISBN 0-07-142273-0 (alk. paper)
    1. Interpersonal communication. I. Title.
HM1166.S48 2004
302.2—dc22

2004006629

Contents

Acknowledgments

When Barry Neville, an editor at McGraw-Hill, first contacted me about writing a book on communication, I was both flattered and concerned. Although I had always loved writing, I had no immediate plans for a book. I did not think the world needed another book on communication skills and I could not imagine what I could write about that hadn't already been written—what tales I could tell that hadn't already been told.

How wrong I was! As I sat down to write, I was amazed at how much I had to say. Although many of the concepts in this book have been addressed before by wonderful, insightful writers, the experience of communicating is deeply personal. As such, each author has a unique perspective. I believe there are two things that differentiate my perspective from others. The first is my contrary nature; conventional wisdom rankles me. The other is my contention that communication is inherently imperfect because it is human. Therefore, efforts to attain perfection are fruitless. More realistic and perfectly respectable is the approach whereby we strive to become good enough. Being good enough allows for the experimentation mentioned above and the pursuit of other interests, both important contributors to overall communication effectiveness, without the pressure and inhibitions bred by the quest for perfection.

So, of course, I first thank Barry Neville, who took a chance on an unknown author, worked closely with me to develop the proposal and sold it to the publisher. Once the manuscript was complete, Barry used his expert eye and instincts to tame what I had written. He was also encouraging along the way, looking at just-written chapters and letting me know whether I was on track. It is not too dramatic to say that without Barry, this book may never have been written.

Denise Marcil, my agent, and her associate, Maura Kye, have always been there to advise and help me, especially during the contract phase and during the final months before publication. They have been particularly encouraging regarding the subject matter and my writing style, since my objectivity has declined with each rereading of the book. I also appreciate that they are pushing me to begin thinking about writing a second book.

Mary Glenn, executive editor at McGraw-Hill, has been very support-ive with both marketing and editorial advice. I especially appreciate Mary's flexibility. Daina Penikas, editing supervisor at McGraw-Hill, and her cadre of copy editors carefully examined my writing to make sure it met McGraw's high standards. Daina's team also conceived of the graphics that appear throughout the book and that make it attractive and easy on the eye. I must also thank Lucy Hedrick, the author and consultant, who introduced me to Denise Marcil and advised me during a difficult period of mental block.

My parents and siblings were, naturally, instrumental in helping me to form my ideas. All of them are genuinely nice people and care about the world around them. Many of the lessons put forth in this book, especially the ones concerning empathy, I learned growing up with them.

My husband, Brad Olsen-Ecker, who is the most talented person I know and who has a sense of humor to match, deserves tremendous credit. Brad is always a source of encouragement and support, both emotional and financial. He is always in a good mood, which is infectious. My daughters Britt and Lily have graciously dealt with my neglect as a work-ing parent and left me alone at critical moments so I could write. They cheered me on, urging me to write more and congratulating me each time I finished a chapter. Their expressions of pride that Mommy could write a book was one of the things that kept me going.

I am especially grateful to my clients who continue to place com-fortable feelings aside and try out my suggestions and recommendations, many of which work as planned—and a few that don't. This takes courage and faith, which I appreciate. I am also indebted to my many friends and colleagues, who, over the years, have given me advice and asked me for my suggestions. There would be no book without these good people, sev-eral of whom are mentioned in these pages.

Preface

The premise of this book is that since others form ideas about us within the first few seconds of meeting, why not employ strategies to establish a good impression and grow it into something that will endure? It is my belief, my creed, that every individual can learn to *get others to see things their way*—to *win them over*. Each and every contact we have with people is an opportunity to inspire, motivate, persuade, and advance business and personal interests. Excellence as a communicator is widely recognized as being synonymous with success. The challenge is being able to accomplish this quickly. This book puts forth tried and true methods for becoming a successful and skilled marketer of self and ideas. Furthermore, it is useful for people in every walk of life, from the company president to the PTA.

In my 15 years as a consultant to large corporations and senior executives, I have often been called on to work with executives on presentation skills and public speaking. Although I continue to do and love this kind of work, several years ago I noticed a need for competency on a deeper level. I discovered that for all the time and money spent helping these hardworking people to develop expertise standing in front of a group and delivering a presentation or speech, their more pressing need was to learn to sell themselves, their companies, and their ideas and to be successful interpersonally within their world. To meet this demand, I developed a practice area devoted to helping corporate employees become better overall communicators, critical abilities that make or break careers.

Get Them to See It Your Way, Right Away is intended as a guide, a reference book, and a motivational treatise on the immense power of good interpersonal communication. Inside is a systematic, step-by-step approach to employing techniques and behaviors designed to help readers quickly organize thoughts and ideas and deliver them with impact. It contains stories from the front as well as methods, tips, tools, and worksheets gleaned and developed during my career working with some of the biggest and most prestigious companies and institutions in this country and internationally. It is also based on relationships with individual employees of these companies that grew as a result of working with them to increase their ability to win over bosses, clients, and colleagues in what has become an extraordinarily competitive business environment.

Perhaps most important, I have attempted to put to rest a persistent myth: the idea that selling—oneself or one's product or service—is phony, slick, or manipulative. I believe now more than ever that selling our ideas and ourselves can and should be invigorating, honest, and authentic. It should demonstrate that we care enough about what others think of us to work at influencing that outcome.

Consultants in my field know all too well that the skills I refer to here are defined by corporations and many individuals as "soft." *Hard skills* are defined as technical knowledge that can be quantified easily and directly affect the bottom line, the work product. Connoted as such, soft skills are not worthy of too much attention—until, that is, it comes time to make hiring decisions or during performance reviews that influence promotions and bonuses. Employees are then left to their own devices to make the required improvements, if they even know what improvements are needed. When discussing its importance, I make clear that the ability to quickly *get others to see things your way* (a soft skill) facilitates delivery of the end product (a hard skill). This ability greatly influences whether ideas are accepted and put into action. It greatly influences business generation. It greatly influences hiring and promotion. In other words, it greatly influences the bottom line. So instead of assigning it the word *soft,* we should look at it for what it is: an essential, professional, difficult-to-acquire skill that directly affects profits.

Although corporate managers usually agree with this, when the time comes to address communication with some training, the time and money necessary to bring about change overwhelm them. This type of training is not like learning a new software program. It takes time—a long time—to change deeply ingrained behaviors. It is poorly understood and can be expensive, and companies naturally are squeamish about spending a lot of money, not to mention employees' time, on something they can't get their arms around. However, when corporations do make a commitment to such employee development, the gains can be tremendous. Jack Welch, the former chairman of General Electric (GE), built one of the world's greatest companies with a winning combination of cutting-edge business practices and professional development programs offered through GE's preeminent corporate university. At GE, employees can learn everything they need to run their businesses and manage their employees—or do their jobs and manage their bosses. During his tenure, Welch was well known to relish the role of classroom teacher and chief provocateur, regularly challenging employees to raise the bar and giving them the helping hand they needed to do it. Jack Welch's power to *get them to see things his way* was legendary.

Although nothing can substitute for good mentoring or direct hands-on supervision such as that provided by GE, my hope is that this book will provide a helping hand, plant a seed or two, and motivate people to get the direct support that they need.

My most successful approach in consulting and training has been to put myself in the shoes of my clients—to get into their hearts and minds and try my best to understand how they may be feeling. I attempt to do this in my writing as well. I have provided numerous examples of clients or friends who have faced tough communication challenges. I also have reached back into my own life and experiences. I have faced most of the situations described in this book myself and have somehow lived to tell about them. *I can empathize.* This empathy reflects my philosophy that to get results, people must be made to feel that they are not alone so that they can feel empowered to try new things.

Get Them to See It Your Way, Right Away is intended to inform a broad readership, as relevant for people new to the workforce as for seasoned managers. It is also useful beyond the workplace. Personal lives have become equally complicated, with relationships tangled as never before. At the same time, we have all experienced an exponential increase in busyness, finding less time to attend to the overwhelming requirements of either work or life. In fact, they are completely intertwined. This book can be used as a way to begin to unravel some of those knots.

The most exhilarating part of creating this book has been how much I have learned by the act of writing it all down. The crystallizing of my thoughts has been invaluable and has made me a much better communicator. Writing has helped me to serve my clients better by making me better able to explain concepts that I had always found difficult to put across.

A few words about how this book is organized: I have tried to be systematic in my delivery of the information, but this does not mean that you must read in order. I do recommend reading Chapters 1 and 2 first because they lay out some basic tenets. After that, it may suit readers to scan the table of contents and jump to chapters that are of specific interest. After each chapter is a list of "Ruth's Truths," which are the most important points in that chapter. I also have taken all 100 of "Ruth's Truths" and listed them at the end of the book. Readers who need some quick reminders or refreshers may find it helpful to scan this section as necessary.

My fondest wish is that this book will promote a new culture of communication, helping people to think differently and deeply about it, dispense with old habits, and form new ones. I believe wholeheartedly that over all objections, people *want* to be *won over—people want to be sold.* They just want and deserve to be presented with interesting concepts and possibilities that will widen their knowledge and, hopefully, their wallets. *Get Them to See It Your Way, Right Away* will show the way.

Get Them to
See It Your Way,
Right Away

Life's a Pitch: Selling Your Ideas to the President or the PTA

I believe with all my heart that we are always pitching, selling ourselves. And I don't believe that this is a bad thing. The simple act of reaching out to people and trying to connect is an act of persuasion. Most of us care whether people like us or not and understand that when we are liked and admired, we are more able to get the things we want. This is a universal truth that is demonstrated repeatedly by successful people. We watch it on TV as those who would be our leaders vie for our votes. We read about it in newspapers—for better and for worse—when laws are made or modified to suit a narrow interest group. We realize that businesses have sent professional lobbyists to influence our politicians, who then pass such laws. We also see it amply demonstrated by those who so expertly raise money and mine resources for good causes. While some of this may be problematic, these successful people, who have elevated their sales pitches to such high art, are enviable in that they have been able to hone their skills to elicit a big payoff. A successful salesperson is a unique commodity and worth her weight in gold.

Unfortunately, selling has gotten a bad reputation. The dictionary definitions that are relevant to this book are "to convince of, to gain acceptance."[1] For many reasons, however, selling also has acquired some unfavorable definitions, such as "to cheat or dupe, a hoax or swindle."[2] It has become associated with being phony and inauthentic, with forcing people to buy things they don't want or need. Surely we have all experienced the humiliation and exasperation of feeling taken for a ride or

1

being suckered. I know that every four years or so I feel that familiar irritation creeping up on me when I listen to presidential candidates trying to sell the electorate on their visions for the country. I get confused and don't know whom to vote for because I don't know whom to believe. I suspect that I've got plenty of company. This is not what I think of when I sell, and this is not where we're going here. Rather, I want to set forth some ideas about selling and pitching that are honest, genuine, and borne of a deep interest in other people.

ANALYSIS OF A PITCH

Recently, I had my first facial. Janna, the aesthetician, was lovely and had a very nice, calm manner of speech and a pleasant speaking voice. She was clearly experienced at putting clients at ease. She exuded confidence as she came to greet me and lead me to the private room where, for the next hour, she would be gently rubbing creams and oils into my face. Her overriding mandate, it seemed, was to make it a very relaxing experience for me. She also wanted to sell me some products. Earning commissions by selling such products is a primary source of income for people in her field. Now, I may never have had a facial, but I am a frequent patron of salons and know the drill. I rarely walk out with anything resembling a shopping bag. But this woman made me feel so good that I ended up buying some products—without asking the price. And I think Janna had me sold *within the first five minutes of our meeting.*

In fact, I was feeling so heavenly on checking out that it did not even register when I looked at the total on my credit card receipt. When I got home (and came down a little bit) and looked at the price I had paid for the products that I had received, I was appropriately stunned. Thank goodness it wasn't a car! Always curious about how such a sale takes shape, I did an analysis. What was it that was so persuasive about Janna?

As I said earlier, Janna put me at ease right away. She was polite but warm and well spoken with a soothing voice and precise pronunciation and articulation. She used this asset to good effect by asking a lot of questions and reassuring me: *"Are you comfortable? Please let me know if you are ever uncomfortable or need something done differently. Have you ever had a facial before? Why not? What do you use to cleanse—not soap?"*

Note that these questions are designed to elicit information about ideas and personal habits so that she could position her product recommendations to me. I will admit to feeling manipulated at certain moments, but her work was so impeccable that it was easy to disregard these feelings. Not insignificantly, the surroundings were plush and luxurious, and although not Janna's doing, they obviously added tremendously to the total experience. I also felt that she had a strong work ethic. Perhaps everyone who gives facials spends an entire hour. But it *felt* as if she were doing more than she had to. And this is a principal quality of people who are adept at getting others to see things their way: *They seek first to give in order to receive.* They exceed expectations.

So what we have here are the basic elements of a successful, honest, and authentic pitch:

1. Janna, the professional with the following traits: warmth, know-how, strong communication skills, product knowledge, a seeming enjoyment of her work, and a strong work ethic
2. The location: beautiful, luxurious surroundings with every comfort provided
3. The client, in this case, me: open to something new and with an unknown need that was skillfully identified

Funny, I had planned originally to have a full body massage, too, but wasn't able to find the time. It's a good thing. The facial was quite enough as a relaxing treatment. A massage would've been overkill. The bottom line was that I liked Janna, and as much as she wanted to please me, *I wanted to please her in return.* While her need was filled by providing a service using all her skills and experience, mine was filled by buying products that she recommended, thus demonstrating that I agreed with her assessments. This mutual satisfaction of needs forms the basis of a sound selling relationship.

Y'GOTTA LIKE PEOPLE

This may sound corny, but it's true. The most successful people love the thrill of meeting new people and getting to know them. It's a challenge to them to see if they can persuade another person to open up, to smile back, to remember them. One of the masters of this skill is our former president, Bill Clinton. Whether you like him or not, this president was and remains a virtuoso of interpersonal communication. During the years that he was in office, I heard it over and over again from people who had met the man: when Bill Clinton shook a hand, it was as if only he and the other person were in the room. Clinton must have recognized early in his political career that he had this effect on people and honed the skill until he had attained mastery. Now some might argue that this particular skill of Clinton was born of low self-esteem or the need to be liked at any cost (true of many). And he most certainly was supremely nongifted in the other essential communication skill of self-awareness. Still, I believe that the man truly liked other people, relished the challenge of meeting them and welcoming them into his fold, cared about them, and was able to put this across interpersonally.

George W. Bush is also quite good at this, which is one very important reason that he defeated Al Gore in 2000. Stories reported from the very beginning of his presidency told about his penchant for assigning nicknames ranging from associates with whom he worked closely all the way to senators. This indicates a fondness for people and an understanding of techniques for breaking down barriers to communication.

There are countless other politicians and celebrities I can name who benefit tremendously from superb interpersonal skills and charisma, which can be defined as great personal magnetism. Politicians such as Ronald Reagan and Elizabeth Dole come to mind, as do television personalities such as Oprah Winfrey, Diane Sawyer, Katie Couric, and the late Charles Kuralt and sports figures, including Michael Jordan, Roger Clemens, and Billie Jean King. Barbara Walters is another good example of someone who is able to break down barriers. Ms. Walters has, for years, been able to persuade some very reluctant celebrities to subject themselves to the most deeply personal questions. To make this happen, Barbara Walters must possess excellent selling skills.

This group of people genuinely seem to have a love for their fellow humans. They come across as having a positive view of life and seem sincerely interested in what others have to say. They radiate confidence and, more significant, make others feel important.

GOOD COMMUNICATORS: MADE, NOT BORN

In considering some of the people just described, it's worthwhile to contemplate whether they were born with any special talents in the area of interpersonal communication. I would argue that there is some merit to the idea that some people are born with temperaments that make them more able to connect with and befriend others. They are often said to have a gift. As we observe those who seem to have what it takes, we frequently end up thinking that it's something that comes naturally or not at all; some people have it, and some don't—it's all or nothing. But this kind of thinking is wrongheaded.

We don't get much, if any, formal training in interpersonal communication as we go through life. It's taught indirectly, if it's taught at all. However, becoming a good communicator is attainable for just about everyone. Think of it as similar to learning to play a musical instrument. Most people who take up the piano have little hope of becoming a Mozart. With practice, though, they will learn to play a Mozart sonata within a relatively short period of time, and they will be able to play for the rest of their lives.

As with gifted musicians, there are gifted communicators. These people command attention and possess magnetism and charisma. Folks like this walk into a room, and people gravitate to them. These appealing people have recognized that excellence as a communicator is synonymous with success. Far from leaving it to nature, however, they work at it, think about it, try new things, and consider these skills to be part of who they are. They know that skilled communicators can inspire, motivate, and persuade others and advance business and personal interests. They understand that they have the best chance of getting what they want and need in life—and meeting their clients' and families' needs—if they use excellent communication skills to influence the people around them. They know that the best route is honest, authentic communication because that method encourages others to do the same. The good news is that like practicing music, systematic and careful communication practice has helped the "less gifted" among us grow into superior communicators with lifelong skills.

"Practice + Experience = Spontaneity"

This anonymous quote is crucial to understanding the process of becoming a terrific communicator. My clients often worry that if they practice and work at it, they'll come across as canned or phony. They think that communication should come naturally; if we are spontaneous, ourselves, then our work or expertise will speak for itself. In fact, it's the opposite; the more practice and experience you have, the greater is your ability to communicate well. By viewing it in this way, we can say that working hard at communicating well goes hand in hand with being authentic, and thus we *are* being ourselves—our *communicating selves*. The key, as in many things, is to become so skilled that it just *looks easy*. Thus, if you feel that you're one of the many people out there who believe that they just weren't born with the right stuff, read on.

FIRST IMPRESSIONS LAST

There is a famous saying: "You never get a second chance to make a first impression." I would add one word to this and say, "You never get a second chance to make a *good* first impression." Every time we interact with other people, we are creating an impression. No matter where we are or what we do or say, those with whom we are communicating are forming ideas about us. These ideas begin to take shape even before we may become aware that we are sending the very signals that color people's perceptions of us. And these impressions are lasting and difficult to alter. Think about it: A person walks into a room, and we immediately size that person up. We think about what that individual's life is like, what he does for a living, how his personal life is, and whether we'd like to get to know him—*immediately*.

Take Responsibility for the Impression You Want to Leave

Doesn't it make sense, then, to take responsibility for helping people form the best possible impression of us? After all, this is how relationships are begun, and good relationships are keys to success in life and business.

Too often people don't accept responsibility for the impressions they make on others. It takes a good deal of planning and energy to implement, and we aren't always successful. That, however, doesn't stop most folks from speaking to each other. They just don't spend much, if any, time thinking about what they would like the outcome to be. I propose another route: a little careful planning can go a good, long way toward a positive outcome, and it doesn't matter if you're a corporate vice president or a member of the PTA.

Deb's Story

A friend of mine, Deb, who had worked for corporations for her entire career, decided to become a teacher. During her years in corporate work, she had learned teamwork, organizational skills, to ask for help when she couldn't go it alone, and very important, the discipline required to get the job done. Thus, when she was hired as an elementary school teacher in a small city, she brought many of those qualities and lessons with her. Now, as any first-year teacher will tell you, that initial year is the most difficult. Not only do you have to start from scratch designing lesson plans, but you also have to contend with getting to know the individual school's culture. This consists of the administrators and other teachers, many of whom have been in their jobs for decades and have very fixed ideas about how things are done. You also must deal with managing the students, who can be very difficult, *and their parents.*

You might think that the job skills that Deb had acquired in her former career would be a good thing—and some of them were. In particular, her ability to be organized was very useful to her as she designed lesson plans and scheduled student activities. Within the first few weeks, however, due to her assertive manner, she made enemies of not only several of her fellow teachers but also the principal and assistant principal. It seems that the direct approach to getting assistance that had worked so well for her in her former position was not working in this new culture. Although she realized this relatively early in the school year, the damage had already been done. She was viewed as aloof and as *not* being a team player or having paid her dues. People became downright nasty and made a difficult job even tougher. Feeling the dislike that emanated from these people made Deb naturally reluctant to attend school social functions, even though there were many coworkers with whom she did have good relationships. This fed their impression that Deb was aloof and thought that she was "better" than the others. The principal took her to task for minor infractions. The assistant principal, under whose purview fell those small but important quality-of-life things such as getting a substitute if a teacher needed a couple of hours off to go to a doctor appointment or to attend her own child's school play, was stingy with that type of relief.

While coaching her during this period, I had to take into consideration that she was my friend and that, as such, I would be biased in her favor. Admittedly, much of what she told me sounded petty. Still, to help her, I needed to be as objective as possible. As we analyzed how this had come to pass, we recognized that the public education culture was a very different environment from what she had been accustomed to. One thing that played a part was the preponderance of women coworkers and leaders and the resulting differences in how they communicated and expected others to communicate. In addition, although all organizations have bureaucracies, the public education bureaucracy, with its government and union affiliations, is one of the most entrenched and difficult to navigate.

After coming to these realizations, Deb changed her tack. Still, it took several months for her to bring around the teachers she had alienated, and it wasn't until the end of the year that she was able to appease the administrators. What should've been a nurturing, supportive environment for a new teacher was instead a combative, difficult one filled with stress. It left such a sour taste in Deb's mouth that she considered abandoning teaching altogether. Fortunately, while she did not return to that school, she did continue at another school, took what she had learned with her, and now loves her job. Had my friend anticipated some of what we discovered during our analysis, she might've had a more pleasant experience. The moral to this story is that it can be very difficult to change a first impression, so you need to do your homework and plan to make a good one.

MICROCOMMUNICATING: SMALL MEETINGS AND INFORMAL ENCOUNTERS RULE

Almost all the communicating we do is on a small scale. It is the exception for most people to give large, formal presentations very often, although they certainly may have to do this occasionally. In reality, most of what we do consists of what I call *microcommunicating*. Microcommunication consists of all the interactions we barely think about and that go on all day long, such as meals with clients and colleagues, seeing the boss in the hall or elevator, stopping into a coworker's office (or vice versa), business social events, professional association meetings and industry gatherings, fundraisers, galas, and other civic-minded get-togethers, not to mention talking on the phone.

Of course, I do not advocate planning and strategizing for every single communication. That would be unnecessary, not to mention exhausting. A few carefully chosen opportunities, however, will create outcomes that have the potential to be life changing. The following chapters will set forth some ideas, tools, and techniques that will make it logical and easy for you to convert everyday communications into opportunities to get bosses, clients, and colleagues, as well as friends and family members, to see things your way.

Ruth's Truths for Chapter 1

Ruth's truth 1: The simple act of reaching out to people and trying to connect is an act of persuasion.

Ruth's truth 2: Selling and pitching should be honest, genuine, and borne of a deep interest in other people.

Ruth's truth 3: People who are adept at selling and winning over others seek first to give in order to receive by doing more than they have been asked to do.

Ruth's truth 4: A sound selling relationship is marked by a mutual satisfaction of needs.

Ruth's truth 5: To be successful at winning over others, y'gotta like people.

Ruth's truth 6: Becoming a good communicator takes careful and systematic practice.

Ruth's truth 7: People form impressions about others within seconds of meeting or speaking with them, and these initial impressions are hard to change.

Ruth's truth 8: Leaving a good impression takes planning.

Set Goals (Because If You Don't Know What You Want, You Won't Get It)

We all set goals. Daydreams are goals. We just are not always successful at realizing them. So it's a good idea to look at why it is important to set goals or objectives. When we set goals, we give ourselves a better chance of getting what we want out of life. Goals can be any size or shape. They can range from having a family with four kids in a big house in a nice suburb to being a chief executive officer (CEO) or a movie star. The most important thing to remember when setting goals is to be realistic. Even here, though, I would caution you not to be realistic to a fault. For example, it would be unrealistic to set a goal of playing professional basketball if you are physically short. However, it would be realistic to a fault if you ruled out a working life in basketball. If you love the game and passionately want to be involved, you could build a career as an executive at the National Basketball Association (NBA) or become an agent for basketball players. You could become a basketball or sports broadcaster or a high school or college basketball coach. (I do not subscribe to the saying that those who can't do, teach. It's hogwash.) Therefore, following your bliss can be achievable as long as it is realistic. Besides, unrealistic goals that are difficult, if not impossible, to achieve are discouraging and sap energy, and that's no good for anyone.

Another thing to remember is that the farther from the present time you set your goal, the more difficult it is to meet it. A good example involves saving for retirement. It's well known that people in their early twenties who begin saving and investing as little as $100 per month, with interest and compounding, will accumulate over $1 million by the time they retire in their sixties. Many young people have the financial wherewithal to save $100 per month. And if $100 is too much, what about $50 or $25? The point is that there is still the potential for a great windfall 40 years hence. Because most 20-year-olds have a hard time imagining life at age 60, however, they do not set the goal or put a plan in place to achieve it. It is too abstract, even though actuarial tables state quite clearly the reality that average life expectancy today for all Americans is somewhere around 76 years. I am certainly an example of someone who while in my twenties could not look that far ahead. In addition, I didn't have this kind of financial information—not that it would have made any difference.

Therefore, in addition to keeping goals realistic, keep them close enough that you can taste them. I'm not saying that the savings plan just described isn't worth exploring. It most certainly is. But looking that far ahead does not work well with many of the other kinds of life and work successes most people are after. Setting goals is very detail-oriented work. For this reason, I recommend writing them down. I have two forms that I use. The first is a simple chart that identifies my goals and sets them in time frames to be achieved: near term (now–1 year), near-medium term (1–3 years), medium term (3–5 years), and far term (5–10 years). The second form is a three-part "Strategies for Success Plan" that serves to help me crystallize my goals and analyze my progress. I like to know why I fail as well as why I succeed. I also spend a lot of time revisiting and revising, as you'll see in part 3 of my "Strategies for Success Plan."

As you think of goals, write them down. And be disciplined about it. I write down goals no matter how ridiculous they may seem at the moment. I can always discard them later. Remember to view them with a somewhat jaundiced eye—Are they realistic, achievable? If not, don't throw them away. Store and review them periodically because in a few weeks or months, goals that seemed impossible suddenly may be within reach.

On the next page is the chart that I use to list my goals and examples of goals that you may want to consider. Be advised that the list and time frames are not set in stone but rather are loose parameters that you may want to consider. In other words, if you reach a goal before you had planned, then you should revise the plan to reflect it. The same holds true for goals that you don't quite manage. They are listed incrementally, and many are intended to be carried through from year to year, not finished and forgotten. For example, the near-term goal of obtaining speaking engagements is something that should be done in each of the four stages. In addition, I've listed goals for entrepreneurs/employees, and personal lives. Many of the goals do double or triple duty.

Goal Examples

TIME FRAME	ENTREPRENEUR/ EMPLOYEE GOALS	PERSONAL/LIFE GOALS
Near-term goals (now–1 year)	1. Decide on business or career	1. Seek out volunteer opportunities
	2. Get a job in career choice	2. Graduate
	3. Develop a business plan	3. Create a personal budget
	4. Design a business logo	4. Go on a diet
	5. Join a business association	5. Get some exercise
	6. Take a class	6. Do community theater
	7. Secure a mentor	7. Take a winter vacation to a warm spot
	8. Network with peers	
	9. Offer services to nonprofit agency	
	10. Identify client base	
	11. Obtain speaking engagements	
	12. Do a mailing	
	13. Create a Web site	

TIME FRAME	ENTREPRENEUR/ EMPLOYEE GOALS	PERSONAL/LIFE GOALS
	14. Write press release for submission to local papers	
	15. Look into and begin certification processes necessary to business	
Near-medium term goals (1–3 years)	1. Head up a committee in a business association	1. Pay off a car loan
	2. Get promoted	2. Continue diet and exercise
	3. Have roster of active clients providing $50,000 to $75,000 in revenue	3. Hone tennis and/or golf games
	4. Outsource clerical work	4. Go to Europe
	5. Enhance Web site by writing monthly articles that require a subscription	5. Fatten savings account
	6. Hire a business coach	
	7. Enroll in graduate school	
	8. Enroll in a long-term professional development program	
	9. Continue speaking engagements	
Medium-term goals (3–5 years)	1. Develop a client base generating $100,000+ in revenue	1. Travel to China

TIME FRAME	ENTREPRENEUR/ EMPLOYEE GOALS	PERSONAL/LIFE GOALS
	2. Write a book	2. Get married
	3. Get graduate degree	3. Have a child
	4. Lead business association	4. Rent a bigger apartment
	5. Hire an assistant	
	6. Get mentioned in a newspaper article	
	7. Get larger office space	
Far-term goals (5–10 years)	1. Be president of a company with 5 to 10 employees	1. Purchase a home
	2. Increase office space again	2. Move to a nice suburb
	3. Write a second book	3. Have two more children
	4. Get promoted to senior vice president	4. Volunteer in child's school
	5. Become a partner in a law firm	
	6. Be a keynote speaker at an industry event	
	7. Mentor someone	
	8. Become a member of the board of directors of a favorite nonprofit	
	9. Donate money to alma mater or other good cause	

Following is a template that you can use to list your own goals:

Goals for Success

TIME FRAME	ENTREPRENEUR/ EMPLOYEE GOALS	PERSONAL/LIFE GOALS
Near-term goals (now–1 year)	_____ _____ _____ _____	_____ _____ _____ _____
Near-medium term goals (1–3 years)	_____ _____ _____ _____	_____ _____ _____ _____
Medium-term goals (3–5 years)	_____ _____ _____ _____	_____ _____ _____ _____
Far-term goals (5–10 years)	_____ _____ _____ _____	_____ _____ _____ _____

MOVING FROM GOALS TO ACTION

What's often missing when we set or imagine goals is the *how*—"How do I get from here to there?" The difference between those who are successful at realizing their goals and those who are not is that successful people formalize their goals. They develop hierarchies of priorities. They write out a plan of action for reaching them because they know that goals can only be reached by solid planning. This is akin to the concept of writing a business plan. In fact, a business plan is full of goals. It is a formal document that describes the way a business intends to meet its marketing and financial goals. The business plan is required, for example, to obtain a loan from a bank. In addition to meeting and assessing the leadership of a business, the bank studies the plan and decides if the goals are realistic and achievable. If so, the bank considers making the loan. It is an essential component of the package.

The plan that I have developed helps successful people meet the goals that are the building blocks of a business or a career. The act of writing things down crystallizes ideas and goals and helps you to plan the steps you must take to achieve them. This leads to action. There is an Irish proverb that aptly says: "You will never plough a field if you have only turned it over in your mind."

Thus, instead of just turning goals over in my mind, I developed the "Strategies for Success Plan" to help put my goals into action. Before starting on the plan, though, begin by remembering the following guidelines that will help your goals take shape:

1. *Describe your goals.*
   - *Must be specific.* Instead of very broad statements such as, "I want to be rich," your goal should be specific, such as, "I want to make a lot of money designing Web sites."
   - *Must stir passion.* What turns you on? If you could accomplish anything at all, what would it be? What do you spend most of your time thinking about and wishing for? Answering these questions will help you to unearth the things you truly desire in life.
   - *Can be any size.* Goals can be large, small, and anything in between. They can be far, medium, or near term. They can be intended to be achieved simultaneously or one by one.

2. *Prioritize.*
   - Decide what is urgent, important, and unimportant.
   - Determine what you can do right now to start down the path to success.
     - Should be achievable.
3. *Act.*
   - Do it.
4. *Revisit and revise.*
   - Keep track of how things are going.
   - Periodically review your plan and assess how you're doing.
   - If things are not going according to the original plan, ask yourself why, decide whether you need to revisit, and if so, revisit and revise.

An important thing to remember is that you must not wait for the planets to be perfectly aligned to set forth on reaching your goals. If you do, it may keep you from moving forward and end up as one of the many excuses you use to procrastinate. So stop filing, surfing the Web, and chitchatting with old friends, and start writing.

On the following pages is my "Strategies for Success Plan" that you can use to help yourself take action and chart your progress. It contains three parts. The first is the view from 30,000 feet and is very general. Part 2 helps you to get specific about actions you can take, and part 3 is designed to help you assess your progress. Modify the plan as necessary. If you get stuck, take a look at some of the examples I provided in the "Goals for Success" form on page 16. In addition, remember that any time a goal comes into your mind, write it down. There is plenty of time to discard it later.

STRATEGIES FOR SUCCESS PLAN

Part 1

What turns me on? What am I passionate about?

_____

_____

What can I do now or near term?
   Within 1–3 weeks?

_____

_____

   Within 1–3 months?

_____

_____

   Within 1 year?

_____

_____

What can I do over the longer term?
   Near medium term (1–3 years):
     Large:

_____

_____

     Small:

_____

_____

     Realistic?

_____

_____

   Medium term (3–5 years):
     Large:

_____

_____

     Small:

_____

_____

     Realistic?

_____

_____

Far term (5–10 years):
　Large:

_____

_____

　Small:

_____

_____

　Realistic?

_____

_____

Part 2: Get Specific

What steps can I take right now to get started?

☐ Name my business　　　　　Done?　☐ Y　　☐ N

　If yes, what? _____

　If no, why not? _____

☐ Call a customer　　　　　　Done?　☐ Y　　☐ N

　If yes, when? _____

　If no, why not? _____

☐ Register for a networking event　Done?　☐ Y　　☐ N

　If yes, what? _____

　If no, why not? _____

☐ Register for a class　　　　Done?　☐ Y　　☐ N

　If yes, what? _____

　If no, why not? _____

☐ Design a logo   Done?   ☐ Y   ☐ N

If yes, what? _____

If no, why not? _____

☐ Speak at an event   Done?   ☐ Y   ☐ N

If yes, what? _____

If no, why not? _____

☐ Other: _____   Done?   ☐ Y   ☐ N

If yes, what? _____

If no, why not? _____

What people can I connect with who potentially can be of help to me?

☐ Customer   Done?   ☐ Y   ☐ N

If yes, who and when? _____

If no, why not? _____

☐ Mentor   Done?   ☐ Y   ☐ N

If yes, who and when? _____

If no, why not? _____

☐ Join an association   Done?   ☐ Y   ☐ N

If yes, what? _____

If no, why not? _____

☐ Volunteer for a committee   Done?   ☐ Y   ☐ N

If yes, what? _____

If no, why not? _____

☐ Other: _____   Done?   ☐ Y   ☐ N

If yes, what? _____

If no, why not? _____

Part 3: Assessment

Have I begun to become more involved in the goals I set forth in part 1?
How? _____
_____
_____

Am I still feeling as passionate about them?   ☐ Yes   ☐ No
Why? _____
_____
_____

Do I need to make adjustments in my goals?   ☐ Yes   ☐ No
What are they? _____
_____
_____

What setbacks have I experienced and why? _____
_____
_____

What new actions or activities can I add to keep up momentum?_____
_____
_____

These three parts of my "Strategies for Success Plan" should keep you on track for a long time. You should get into a habit of constantly tweaking the plan, improving it, honing it, and fine-tuning it until it becomes second nature and part of your business habit. In addition, although the plan is worded with the entrepreneur in mind, I encourage you to change the language to suit your particular situation.

REACH LARGER GOALS BY ACCOMPLISHING SMALLER GOALS

Setting goals is essential to reaching them. Still, a lot of people get stuck, and when you get stuck, you risk becoming distracted and drifting off course. One of the problems that can lead to getting stuck is setting goals that may be too lofty and insurmountable. To avoid getting stuck, therefore, I include all the small things that I do every day as part of my goal-setting activity. This requires some carefully thought out communication. Here are some examples of small goals:

1. I'm going to speak up at the meeting just for the sake of being heard. (Believe it or not, there are worse reasons!)
2. I'm going to set up an appointment to meet _____.
3. I'm going to deliver information that is critical to the outcome of the project.
4. I'm going to object to a strategy that I expect to be raised and describe an alternative that I think will work better.
5. I'm going to introduce myself to _____ at the meeting because she (or he) is someone I should meet and who should meet me.
6. I'm going to walk out of the meeting with the business (or the job offer).
7. The next time I encounter the president of my company, I'm going to strike up a conversation.
8. I'm going to call that recruiter to let him know that I'm still interested in a new position.
9. I will go to the association event tonight so that I can practice doing my introductory pitch.

There are endless examples that can be added to this list. All New Year's resolutions can be counted as goals, including the personal ones such as losing a few pounds or starting to exercise. Again, as you think of them, write them down. It's like a to-do list. All the examples that I provided above have communication as their common theme. These communication strategies facilitate the larger goals. Think of them as steps on a staircase with the main goal at the top.

Ruth's Truths for Chapter 2

Ruth's truth 9: Set goals to give yourself the best chance of getting what you want out of life.

Ruth's truth 10: Write down goals and plans for achieving them.

Ruth's truth 11: Revisit and revise as needed.

Ruth's truth 12: Set smaller goals as incremental steps to larger ones.

3

Speak Loudly (Without Saying a Word, Ssshhh . . .)

In Chapter 1, I noted the existence of charismatic people who command attention with the simple act of walking into a room. I think that it pays to try to identify the characteristics that make them so appealing because you may be thinking that this kind of personal charm is intangible. I disagree and think that there are several concrete characteristics that can be distinguished. Let's start with what is *not* important:

1. Good looks
2. A beautiful speaking voice
3. Expensive clothing
4. Expensive jewelry
5. An expensive car
6. An elite university degree (also expensive)

Perhaps you can come up with several people you know who are charismatic without having any of these supposed advantages. However, you may be thinking: Doesn't that add to the argument that charisma is intangible? Not at all. We just don't spend enough time analyzing what the characteristics are that do work and then trying them on for size.

Below are some traits charismatic people have that are attainable by just about everyone:

1. Exceptional nonverbal communication skills (posture, stance, stride, body movement, eye contact, facial expression, voice, and so on)
2. Appropriate dress and adornment
3. Excellent conversation skills
4. Good listening skills
5. Good grooming
6. A high level of preparation

But wait, you say, there are countless successful people who seem to lack all of the preceding. What about them?

I am reminded of a personal story. Several years ago I was asked to give a presentation to a group of businesspeople. The organization that invited me to speak consisted of a fairly high-powered crowd because the community, located in the metropolitan New York City area, is home to a large number of multinational corporations. These companies are members of the organization, as are other, smaller businesses consisting of owners and employees wishing to network and do business with their larger counterparts.

My topic was presentation skills, a favorite of mine, and I worked long and hard to prepare for the occasion. In such a speech, one area I spend a good proportion of time on is nonverbal communication.

The turnout was large, and I felt that the presentation went well, and this was confirmed by the high evaluations. The organizers were pleased, and I went back to my office happy and with a fresh crop of new contacts. I couldn't wait to start mining this gold. The next day a letter arrived in the mail from one of the attendees. This person took exception to my premise on nonverbal communication, which states that it greatly enhances communication by giving our words meaning (see Chapter 11). As proof that my argument was flawed, he noted that Henry Kissinger and Alan Greenspan didn't have to "wave their arms around" to get noticed.

At first, I was upset. I'm one of those people who wants everyone to like me, and when they don't, I feel that I've done something wrong. The disgruntled attendee also had sent a copy of his letter to the organization. Thus it was nice when a representative of the organization called me after receiving the letter to reassure me that this was not the first time that this individual had complained. The organization was, in fact, pleased with the presentation and had gotten good feedback from many of the attendees.

Still, I take criticism very seriously. Very often there is truth to what is said, and I know that paying attention to it is a good way to improve my skills. I mulled over the comments and came to a conclusion. Would that we all had the fame and renown of either a Henry Kissinger or an Alan Greenspan! These individuals and others of similar status have but to open their mouths for there to be rapt attention. The very nature of their position and name recognition endows them with an automatic level of importance that is impossible for ordinary people to compete with. According to Diane DiResta in her book, *Knockout Presentations*, the continuing argument about style versus substance or, as she puts it, "sizzle versus steak," can be broken down as follows: "You can get away without the 'sizzle' only if you're a celebrity or you're a known expert."[1]

Now, would I, as a professional communicator, be happier if Kissinger and Greenspan were more skilled at the art of speaking, if they had more "sizzle"? Do I think they'd be even more successful if they spoke more expressively and "waved their arms around" a little more? My answer, as my teenage daughter would say, is "Uhh, yeah!" (A confession: I was glad when Mr. Kissinger relinquished a position he had been appointed to by President George W. Bush because I was unhappy at the prospect of listening to that droning voice on the nightly news again.) But must they employ these skills to get attention? Of course not. However, a high level of preparation—see number six on the list of attainable traits— is something the Greenspans and Kissingers of the world have down to a science and regularly apply to their presentations. This is the single most important—and most neglected—trait employed by would-be communicators. This high level of preparation makes them much more expert than their public personas let on.

I do not argue in this book that skilled communication is the only path to success. But I strongly contend that for most ordinary people who are competing in a crowded field, careful, effective nonverbal communication is necessary to cut through the noise and the clutter to gain attention.

BUILDING PERSONAL APPEAL

All the foregoing sets the stage for how we build personal appeal. And like building anything, we must take a systematic, well-planned approach. A good first step is to take a personal inventory. The following form is something I ask clients to complete:

Personal Impact Inventory

What are my general objectives in communicating?

1. _____
2. _____
3. _____
4. _____

What is my general level of confidence?

☐ Excellent   ☐ Good   ☐ Fair   ☐ Poor

How do I rate my appearance?

Dress:

☐ Excellent   ☐ Good   ☐ Fair   ☐ Poor

Adornment (includes jewelry, hair, and makeup):

☐ Excellent   ☐ Good   ☐ Fair   ☐ Poor

How do I rate my nonverbal skills?

Voice (volume, vocal power, rate/pace, expression, vocal tone/quality):

☐ Excellent   ☐ Good   ☐ Fair   ☐ Poor

Diction (pronunciation, accent, dialect, and so on):

☐ Excellent   ☐ Good   ☐ Fair   ☐ Poor

Physical presence (energy, hands, body movements, posture):

☐ Excellent   ☐ Good   ☐ Fair   ☐ Poor

Eye contact/facial expression (animation, smile):

☐ Excellent   ☐ Good   ☐ Fair   ☐ Poor

What nonverbal skills do I need to work on?

1. _____
2. _____
3. _____

How will I accomplish this?

☐ Informal coaching (nonpaid)

☐ Formal coaching (paid)

How do I rate my listening skills?

☐ Excellent ☐ Good ☐ Fair ☐ Poor

What is my customary level of preparation?

☐ Excellent ☐ Good ☐ Fair ☐ Poor

How do I prepare?

_____

_____

The important thing to remember when completing the "Personal Impact Inventory" is to be very honest with yourself. This is extremely difficult to do because it means taking stock of some particularly personal issues. In fact, it may be useful to have someone, such as a trusted friend, colleague, or family member, to help you complete it. Whoever it is, the person should not be afraid to give you honest feedback. That person also should not be unduly harsh.

The Charm Offensive

Being charming is a characteristic that is usually viewed positively. The exception is when it's paired with a negative trait or antisocial behavior, as in a "charming liar" or "He charmed the pants. . . . " Well, you know where I'm going with that one. Charm makes others feel good. It has its genesis in the admiration or genuine liking of other people and the wish to make them feel good. I referred to it in Chapter 1 in the discussion about well-known people who had terrific interpersonal skills. Being able

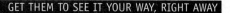

to walk into a room, approach a stranger, introduce yourself, and generate interesting (and interested) conversation is what being charming is all about. And I pair it with the word *offensive* because it's something that has a proactive element to it. Being charming takes planning. The next section will get you started.

TAKE *A.I.M* (ATMOSPHERE, IMPRESSION, MOOD)

> *Even if you're on the right track, you'll get run over if you just sit there.*
>
> —Will Rogers

Whenever clients complain to me that they are skittish about approaching others or initiating a discussion, whether it be a one-on-one discussion with a boss or client, a group discussion with coworkers, or approaching people at networking events, I advise them to take *A.I.M.* Taking *A.I.M.* helps you to think through the initial strategy for establishing communication by focusing on three elements of any interaction: *atmosphere, impression* and *mood.* I developed this tool for myself because, although I enjoy getting together with people, I had found it quite difficult to introduce myself to someone new or insert myself into an existing conversation. Now, unless you know everyone who is going to be at an event or are the first to arrive at an event and stand at the door meeting and greeting everyone who comes in after, you will find yourself in a position where you may have to join conversations that are already in progress.

    A.I.M. can be broken down as follows:

Atmosphere	Analyze the climate, including the environment and people, as well as anticipating potential objections, and decide on the objective you wish to accomplish.
Impression	Look hard at yourself, and settle on an image you want to project.
Mood	Set the tone of any interaction.

The great thing about *A.I.M.*, I have found, is that it can be adjusted to fit other types of situations. Let's look at some typical scenarios and put *A.I.M.* to work:

Scenario 1: Paul would like to ask his boss for a promotion. He takes *A.I.M.!*

Atmosphere	I've been here for three years and gotten decent reviews and raises each year. I worked on a big project that was completed recently and received accolades for my work. I really like my job and the company and would like to grow in my profession. I get along with my boss. I have good performance reviews. The only roadblock I see is that there may be a cap on promotions, or she may be reluctant to give me one at an off time in the fiscal year.
Impression	I want to project an image of strength and confidence but not come across as too aggressive. I do have to guard against being too passive, though. I'm in the one-down position, after all. I'll certainly dress with this in mind. At this juncture, I don't want to consider the possibility of being turned down and don't think I need to—yet. I do not have a plan in place in case of rejection and do not want to leave the job. Also, my boss may think that I'm bucking for a raise (which would be nice) at the same time. The truth is that I'd take the promotion without a raise for the time being. I don't think I'll share that right away.
Mood	I'm thinking about asking her out for lunch so that we're on neutral ground. I know her favorite restaurant. I could send her an e-mail but think I'll approach her in person because I think it's stronger—shows more guts. I'll tell her I want to discuss a couple of things like the new project that's in the pipeline; I guess now I'll have to come up with some ideas about that one.

Scenario 2: Cindy is a business owner who is going to a networking event. She takes *A.I.M.!*

Atmosphere	This is a great organization that I've been eager to check out. I've met a couple of members who have encouraged me to come to an event. I like them. I've seen press coverage, gone to the organization's Web site, and think it'll be a good fit for my business and me. The event is taking place at a local restaurant that should be easy to get to. I've been active with other organizations and could become active with this one. The organization is always looking for good people to be on committees and lead efforts.
Impression	I plan to walk in confidently, even though I won't know a soul (with the exception of those two people who may not even be there). I'll wear my blue pantsuit.
Mood	The first thing I'll plan to do is meet the president. In fact, I'll give him a call or send an e-mail first to introduce myself, let him know I'm coming, and ask if he'll help me out by introducing me to some others. (That'll solve the problem of not knowing a soul.)

Scenario 3: Joanne is a mother who is planning to attend and speak at a school board meeting regarding an issue of great importance to her. She takes *A.I.M.!*

Atmosphere	The meeting is taking place in the auditorium at the new middle school. I've been there—it's gorgeous. The fact that it's there means that they expect a big turnout. I will be seeing several neighbors and people I know, some of whom agree with my point of view and some of whom don't. There is potential for argument and things getting out of hand. I think I'd better anticipate that this could happen and come up with some response strategies just in case.
Impression	I'm going in fully armed with information I've gathered over the past few months. I will, however, not allow my passion for the subject to get in the way of my objectivity.

	I also don't want to wimp out if others go on the attack. I'll practice my talk and rehearse answers to the possible attacks or objections. I'll dress casually, but no jeans.
Mood	Most people read verbatim from a script when they address the board. I'm going to use notes in outline form so that I can look up and speak in a more conversational tone, make eye contact, and come off as friendly and wanting to work together. It's hard to say when I'll be up and what will have transpired already, so perhaps I should even come up with a humorous story or good quote that will break the ice.

All three of these examples are real. The people who used this tool were amazed at how well it smoothed their way toward their communication goal. As with all the tools and techniques in this book, the more you use them, the easier and more natural they become. Try taking *A.I.M.* the next time you have something important to say.

Take *A.I.M.!*

Atmosphere	Analyze the climate. Identify the players and what's in it for them. Assess potential objections or roadblocks. Determine your objective.
Impression	Decide on the image you want to project and how.
Mood	Establish the tone you would like to set and how.

Ruth's Truths for Chapter 3

Ruth's truth 13: The most important traits of charismatic people do not cost money to acquire.

Ruth's truth 14: Preparation is the single most important and single most neglected communication skill.

Ruth's truth 15: Take *A.I.M.* Thoroughly analyze and plan before entering the situation.

May I Have Your Attention, Please!

In Chapter 3, I listed a number of things that figure prominently into commanding attention that anyone can acquire. In this chapter I will discuss how there comes a point in everyone's life when questions get raised about how different things might be "if I were a little more outgoing, if I had taken that opportunity to give that presentation, if I had been better at delivering it, or if I only had discussed this problem with my spouse or close friend before it got out of hand." These are moments of truth that either send people running for cover or act as wake-up calls that you had better change course so that you can increase your chances of success.

As Daniel Goleman puts it in his book, *Working with Emotional Intelligence,* there is a "hard case for soft skills."[1] Goleman notes that in survey after survey of large corporations, "IQ takes second position to emotional intelligence in determining outstanding job performance."[2] And Goleman is very clear that emotional intelligence is not about being nice or touchy-feely, nor is it gender-specific. He defines *emotional intelligence* as the ability to manage feelings—one's own and those of others in a way that creates environments for success.

GETTING NOTICED IN A NOISY WORLD

You may be wondering what all the foregoing has to do with getting attention. Well, the world is a noisy place, and the decibel level is increasing exponentially. I define *noise* as anything that distracts from communication, ranging from the sound of jackhammers at the construction site across the street, to a lack of sleep, to nagging worries, both personal and business. Work has become so much harder over the years, and although we are more productive than at any time in history, we are also putting in many more hours, resulting in many more demands on our time.

The Work Does Not Speak for Itself (It Can't)

I was called on to coach a middle-level executive at a large financial institution. As is almost always the case, I was told that he was very smart and did his job well, but to move up in the organization (and as with so many companies, it is either up or out), he would need to be more successful at internal networking and building relationships. By the way, whenever I'm told that prospective coaching clients are smart, I read that as code for good at the technical skills and not so good at the interpersonal communication skills. As Daniel Goleman notes, it's a different way of being smart.

When I began to meet with Stan, he couldn't understand what he was doing wrong. He was an interesting and nice person and felt bad that he had been singled out for "fixing." He spoke of working very hard, which to him meant putting in a lot of hours completing projects that he was assigned, going to continuing-education classes offered by the company to keep up with trends in the marketplace and to hone his skills, and generally doing his bosses' bidding. Performance reviews, insofar as technical output was concerned, were always good. As Stan remarked in one of our first meetings, "The work speaks for itself." I stopped him and asked him how the work did that. What did it say? And no, I was not trying to be a smart aleck; I was just trying to get to the heart of the matter by playing devil's advocate. Stan was very earnest (and a bit defensive) when he reasserted his view that how he accomplished his tasks was the only thing that should matter regarding performance. I began my campaign to persuade him otherwise by asking some questions, such as

- Did he think it was important to have good relationships with his boss and colleagues? Why?
- What did such good relationships look like?
- What did it take to develop good relationships?

As he began to mull over his responses to these questions, he began to see that his work product, his technical output, was only part of the picture. He needed to promote himself internally—to do some personal marketing. At that point we moved on to questions designed to delve a little deeper:

- Did he think that he already had good relationships with his bosses and coworkers? Could they be any better?
- If so, what steps could he take to improve them?
- How did he feel about doing some self-promotion?

As we moved through our discussion, it became clearer to Stan that not only did he need to put in time on the work itself—the research and analysis that was in his job description and that he was very skilled at—but he also needed to tend to and build his relationships at work in order to promote his skills internally. Slowly he began doing this. I provided Stan with a checklist of relationship-building techniques to which he could refer (see following page). Gradually, he began to adjust his approach to his coworkers. This has to be done slowly and carefully. Many people are taken aback when they are approached in ways that are new. In essence, you are presenting a new face to coworkers and asking them to change some habits of thinking about you. Changing habits takes time. In addition, for Stan and many people, the idea of self-promotion or selling themselves makes them squeamish. They associate it with being slick, insincere, and not genuine, as I described in Chapter 1. Building relationships is not an easy thing to do and does not show results overnight. It takes planning and forethought. If done well, however, it can be very successful.

Stan, I am happy to report, was able to shed some of his old notions and habits and improve his relationships significantly. It took him about nine months, six of which we worked together in person and on the phone. At his next review, he was promoted to vice president. There also was a benefit he hadn't expected: He became happier, felt more at home at work, and enjoyed the relationships he had built.

Relationships: The Foundation of Self-Promotion

The squeamishness that people feel about promoting themselves and their interests has at its core a level of reluctance to build relationships. When relationships are solid and comfortable, opportunities to discuss oneself and one's accomplishments arise naturally. In another situation, a client, Ron, had been passed over for promotion in favor of someone who had accomplished much less (this often happens). When Ron went to ask his boss why he had not gotten the promotion, the boss responded by asking Ron what he had done to merit this type of recognition. Ron was floored by this response. He thought the boss would know about all the work he had done. During our discussions, it came out that the person who had been promoted had cultivated a good relationship with their mutual boss and had been very vocal about the work she had done. Ron admitted that he had not spent any time touting his accomplishments or cozying up to the boss. He has since learned to keep his superiors up to date on what he is doing. He also has created opportunities to socialize informally and build relationships in which tooting his own horn is a natural outgrowth. As a result, he has gotten several good promotions and the nice raises that go with them.

Getting going with the relationship building that is the foundation of self-promotion can be difficult because it involves changing some fairly ingrained habits. The following checklist should help:

Relationship-Building Checklist

Building Relationships with Colleagues

- Offer your help with a project.
- Send interesting articles and lend relevant books you've read.
- Give appropriate compliments about personal appearance* and especially about job performance.
- Invite a coworker and a guest to dinner at your home.
- Stop by a coworker's office to discuss a business issue or ask for advice.
- Invite a colleague to join you for breakfast, lunch, or drinks or coffee after work (in that order).
- Offer to help with a problem a colleague is facing.
- Confide in a coworker about a type of personal, but not intimate, challenge you're facing (self-disclosure).

Building Relationships with Superiors (Initial Efforts)

- Offer your help with a project outside your immediate sphere, even if it means putting in more time.
- Do unexpected work (surprise them).
- Send interesting articles and lend relevant books you've read
- Ask a superior for advice.
- Follow up on a project with an informal, in-person status report.
- Make suggestions about how you could do a better job for the group (e.g., enroll in a class, purchase software, or brainstorm team-building activities).
- Confide in a superior about a type of personal, but not intimate, challenge you're facing (self-disclosure).

Building Relationships with Superiors (Secondary Efforts)

- Invite a superior to lunch.
- Invite a superior for drinks or coffee after work.
- Invite a superior and a guest to dinner at a restaurant.
- Invite a superior and a guest to dinner at your home.[†]

[*]Must be delivered very carefully so as not to be misconstrued or deemed inappropriate.
[†]This requires a relationship that has been growing positively for some time.

A final thought about building relationships with others: Don't forget about the people who report to you. Direct reports as well as secretaries and other support personnel have more power than is generally recognized and can make their bosses' lives either easier or more difficult. I have had numerous clients who, due to poor relationships with direct reports or support staff, have had a good deal of difficulty getting their work done. It's amazing how much work these employees can relieve you of. And when they're feeling ignored or poorly treated, guess who ends up doing their work? A real benefit to having good relationships with your direct reports is that they can offset those extra hours you spend building relationships with your colleagues and bosses. Therefore, remember birthdays, treat them to a nice lunch occasionally, and give holiday gifts. Be generous. As a result of feeling appreciated, most will go the extra mile to make your life easier.

Be Revealing: Exposing and Disclosing

You will notice that in relationships with both colleagues and superiors, I mention the idea of being self-disclosing. This is difficult and risky, but if you are careful about what and how you share, the rewards can be great. It is a crucial building block in the process. When we build relationships, we attempt to build a degree of closeness. We cannot accomplish this unless we are willing to reveal a little about ourselves. What things are safe to discuss that give the right degree of self-disclosure without getting into the category of too much information? The following are potential avenues that lead to relationship building:

- Hobbies or other interests outside work
- Surface issues concerning family
- Current events (be careful when bringing up religion and politics)
- A favorite vacation
- Your favorite TV show
- An embarrassing thing that happened to you that you can look back on and laugh about now

As you get to know someone, your self-disclosure can become deeper, such as

- Religion or politics
- General feelings about work and friendships
- Times when you've had bad things happen but overcame them
- Lessons you have learned

Finally, close relationships can withstand and benefit from a third level of disclosure:

- Deeply personal feelings about work and family
- Hopes and desires for the future
- Worries and concerns about business and personal life

Subtract Distractions

As I discussed in detail earlier in this chapter, the notion that being able to communicate well is a "soft" skill, not worthy of much attention and certainly not as important as the technical or "hard" skills that comprise the work product, is bunk. Certainly, Stan, the financial executive, fell prey to this misconception. One of the most frustrating aspects of my work with corporate executives is contending with this notion. It's interesting, therefore, that when I walk into a seminar or workshop, I sense tension, a deep discomfort, and worry on the part of the participants. These are significant distractions. They don't seem to want to be there (especially in small group workshops where they know they are going to be asked to perform individually a good deal). As a result of these distractions, their ability to maintain the open mind necessary to learn and perform well is impaired. It also has another interesting effect: It belies the notion of communication as being "soft." Once again, Daniel Goleman writes

> In a national survey of what employers are looking for in entry-level workers, specific technical skills are now less important than the underlying ability to learn on the job. After that, employers listed:
> 1. Listening and oral communication
> 2. Adaptability and creative responses to setbacks and obstacles
> 3. Personal management, confidence, motivation to work toward goals, a sense of wanting to develop one's career and take pride in accomplishments
> 4. Group and interpersonal effectiveness, cooperativeness and teamwork, skills at negotiating disagreements
> 5. Effectiveness in the organization, wanting to make a contribution, leadership potential [3]

All these qualities require—and in fact are themselves—communication skills. Even if people are reluctant to consider the importance of these things or, more likely, are not even conscious of them, they still exist at some level of their awareness. Buried knowledge nags at the psyche. We know that these things are true but we don't know what to do about them. So we keep sweeping them under the rug. However, we're constantly reminded of these things each time we have to go to workshops that require us to face our demons and each time we see a successful person. The truth is that the most successful people understand the immense value of these qualities, and this knowledge exists at the forefront of their awareness instead of being submerged.

Use a Little T.L.C. (Tender Loving Criticism)

A major component of working with others is the ability to empathize, to put yourself in the shoes of others to try to understand how they might be feeling. I was working for a large international nonprofit agency delivering a series of workshops encompassing the full gamut of communication and presentation skills. The group was terrific, and I had a great time working with them. They were self-conscious like most attendees at my workshops. Thus my first task when I am conducting a workshop of nervous and self-conscious people is to try to put them at ease. I introduce myself to each participant, shake hands, make a lot of small talk before we get started, use as much good humor as possible, and generally attempt to let them know that we're all in this together. I let them know that I plan to make every effort to create a supportive environment and make the day enjoyable. The overriding technique I use is to continually drive home the reality that I have walked in their shoes, that I wasn't born this way, that it's not a miracle from God that I can speak and communicate well, and that I am always working on it, trying to find new ways to improve. This method of joining with participants, a kind of experiential mind meld, is one of the most effective of all the techniques I can offer to clients. In addition, throughout my workshops, when I have people perform for others and I deliver feedback and critiques, I do it gently and remain mindful of how they may be feeling. Since this is done one by one, I must read each personality separately from the others and deliver information to that person in a way that works for them, that gives them ways to improve that is not humiliating. I surmise how they may be feeling by imagining how *I* would be feeling in a similar situation. By the way, the key here is not imagining how you would feel if you were you but how you would feel if you were the other person, based on what you already know about that person.

By the end of the series of workshops for the nonprofit, I was approached by one of the participants who wanted to tell me how much she had enjoyed the work and how much she had taken away. She also wanted me to know that she had a name for the way I delivered feedback to the participants: *T.L.C.—Tender Loving Criticism*. I thought that was a wonderful compliment and one that I truly took to heart, and I have remembered it and referred to it year after year.

Getting noticed in a noisy world includes a series of communicative behaviors:

- *Speak for your work* (because it can't speak for itself) by building relationships with your bosses and colleagues conducive to self-promotion.
- *Don't ignore support staff and direct reports.*
- *Fashion a plan based on the "Relationship-Building Checklist"* (see page 38).
- *Allow for some self-disclosure.*
- *Subtract distractions* by making efforts to put people at ease via small talk and good humor.
- *Use empathy.* Put yourself in others' shoes and try to imagine how they feel.
- *Deliver feedback gently* and with *T.L.C.—Tender Loving Criticism.*
- *Be supportive.*
- *Be reliable.*
- *Be patient.* Developing the techniques necessary to get noticed takes time.

Ruth's Truths for Chapter 4

Ruth's truth 16: IQ is less important in business than emotional intelligence.

Ruth's truth 17: Relationships are the foundation of self-promotion.

Ruth's truth 18: Build relationships with people at all levels of the organization.

Ruth's truth 19: Self-disclosure is a catalyst to building relationships.

Ruth's truth 20: You must be able to regularly articulate and promote accomplishments; otherwise, people won't know what you've been up to.

Ruth's truth 21: Put yourself in others' shoes before attempting to criticize or give feedback.

5

Who's Buying?

Whenever I am about to meet someone new, and it is something I can plan for (unlike running into someone by accident), I like to know as much as possible about who they are and what makes them tick. And information abounds. As you will see in the following pages, there are many ways to obtain this information. Much information can be gotten without ever leaving your desktop computer. At other times, the personal touch is required. This chapter will show you ways to investigate and plan for the communication experience. First, you have to do an assessment by finding answers to some questions. I have divided them into three categories that are covered in detail in this chapter and the following two chapters: the *Encounter,* the *Encountered,* and the *Encounterer.*

The Encounter[1]

1. What is the occasion? For example, is it an informal or impromptu meeting with boss, a sales call, a volunteer opportunity, a board meeting, a networking event, a keynote speech, a panel presentation, or a political campaign?
2. Is there a program, and if so, what is the schedule?
3. What is the venue?
4. Where is it located?
5. How long do you expect the encounter to last?
6. What is the time of day of the event: morning, afternoon, or evening?
7. Will there be a meal or some other type of food service?
8. Will alcohol be served?

The Encountered

1. Who will be there?
2. How many will be there?
3. What do they have in common
4. What is their background: education, religion, politics, or professional level?
5. What is their average age?
6. What is the gender makeup of your audience?
7. How much do they already know about your topic?
8. Why are they going?

The Encounterer

1. What is your role?
2. Will you be working alone or with a team? If a team, who are they, and what are their roles?
3. Why are you going?
4. What do you want to accomplish?

KNOW YOUR AUDIENCE

This chapter will focus on the second part of the equation: the *Encountered.* Finding out about the people you will be coming into contact with is an excellent way to give yourself a very good chance of meeting your goals. Most people don't take the time to analyze this aspect of the communication equation. It still amazes me when people work so hard to get a meeting with a prospective client, are granted time, and then kick back and relax, thinking that their work is done. For me, once I get the meeting, that's when the real work begins.

REMOTE VERSUS DIRECT COMMUNICATION

Not even 10 years ago I would have to go to the local library and log onto their computer databases to get useful information about companies or business executives I wanted to approach. And this was a terrific thing at the time, because 10 years prior to that I had to wade through book volumes of company listings, hoping things hadn't changed too much. In addition, it seemed that every time I went to the library, someone else was using the book I needed! It was very frustrating and not very productive.

As with so much else, the Internet has revolutionized the way we can obtain information. Almost all organizations and/or business entities—companies, associations, clubs, and so on—have Web sites. And anyone who wants to communicate with these entities should take advantage of the World Wide Web for access to information about them. These Web sites most often contain the following basic information:

- Services/products the company provides
- Information about the leadership
- Press releases
- Client list
- Contact information

In a more sophisticated use of the Internet, companies can sell their products and services 24 hours a day, 7 days a week. No longer is it necessary to wait until Monday at 9 A.M. Pacific Standard Time for someone on the East Coast to buy a product or service located on the West Coast. This has revolutionized marketing and has enriched those who know how to make the best, most efficient use of it.

Any type of information can be added to a company's Web site, such as

- Articles that have been published
- Video files of media appearances or presentations by the leadership
- Audio files of company conference calls (telephone presentations to the financial community)
- Testimonials from satisfied clients
- E-newsletters or e-zines that provide interesting or helpful information to clients and subscribers (access to these may be free of charge but usually requires a subscription so that information about the interested party can be captured and added to the database)
- Online surveys for workshop or seminar participants

Web sites also can be automated to an incredible extent, capturing information, booking business, selling products, and responding to clients any time of the day or night without direct human involvement. Again, businesses that have taken this type of control enjoy a huge advantage.

On my own Web site I have an online survey to make it easy for clients to send me information about their individual needs. Before a workshop or seminar, I send prospective attendees an e-mail with a link to the survey page. They complete the survey online and click the "Submit" button. This sends the information directly to me so that I can analyze clients' responses and tailor my program to best suit their individual or collective needs. (The body of the e-mail is composed to introduce me and the company, put participants at ease, and tell them what to expect and about any prework they need to do or materials to bring.)

The following shows the home page of my Web site ruthsherman.com and an example of my online survey. This one is designed for a workshop on presentation skills.

The benefits of this type of instrument are enormous. It is easy for the client to complete, can be done at the client's convenience, and is

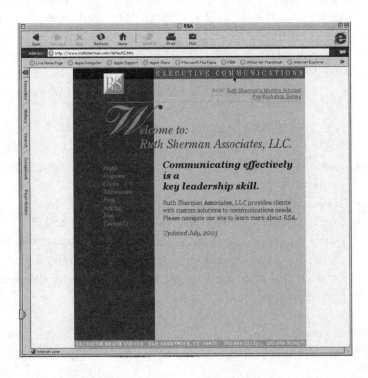

Pre-Workshop Survey

This questionnaire is designed to help us prepare a customized workshop.

Please answer the following questions. Be as detailed as possible and return to us by pressing the SUBMIT button at the end of this survey.

Name/Title:

Your E-Mail Address:

Please describe your job responsibilities:

What are your objectives/goals in participating in the workshop?

Have you had any prior training in presentation skills or public speaking?
  ☐ Y ☐ N
If yes, please describe:

Check your typical presentation situation:
  ☐ Standing presentation
  ☐ Seated presentation
  ☐ Formal speech
  ☐ Workshop/Seminar
  ☐ Other
Please add any details below:

How many people are usually in your audience?
  ☐ 1–5   ☐ 6–10   ☐ 10–20
  ☐ 20–50   ☐ More than 50

What types of visual support, if any, do you use in your presentation?
(Flip charts, overheads, laptops, LCDs, other hardware, software)

How much notice do you receive in advance of doing a presentation?
☐ 1 day or less   ☐ 2–5 days   ☐ 1–2 weeks
☐ 2–4 weeks   ☐ a month or more

Please discuss how you prepare for a presentation:

Please discuss any feelings of stage fright or nervousness you feel prior to and during a presentation and how you feel it affects your performance:

Tell us about some of your presentation strengths:

At the end of this program, what would you like to be able to do differently?

Think carefully about your typical presentation situation. Of the choices below, which ones would have the most value for you to work on during the workshop? (You may check more than one)

☐ Nonverbal skills (hands, body, eyes, face, voice, etc.)
☐ Handling nervousness
☐ Preparation and rehearsal techniques
☐ Staying on message
☐ Handling questions and objections confidently
☐ Seated presentations
☐ Standing presentations
☐ Effective design of visual aids
☐ Effective use of visual aids
☐ Team presentations
☐ Facilitation skills (leading workshops/seminars)
☐ Formal speeches

Please share any additional comments:

instantly transmissible and tremendously helpful to the vendor in meeting clients' needs.

While I love my Web site survey and have found it to be a great help, it does not substitute for direct face-to-face or voice-to-voice interviews. In fact, when I hold workshops, if at all possible, I conduct personal interviews as part of the process. And if, for example, practical considerations such as distance or time-zone differences interfere, I speak to my clients on the phone. In either case, two equally important things are accomplished: (1) an accurate assessment is done, and (2) rapport is built. As I mentioned in Chapter 4, is it common for employees to feel uncomfortable or concerned about being asked to participate in a workshop or seminar. This is my chance to get to know them and have them get to know me before we actually meet. In person, I can read all the nonverbal codes of communication and use them to enhance my understanding of answers to my questions. Not as much can be covered in a phone conversation, in which the nonverbal codes are limited to vocal traits. However, the phone is still far better than remote communication. Direct communication is also more conducive to spontaneous discourse. Many times I have gone in with certain questions and received unexpected responses that led to new questions that shed light on an area neither party had considered. Some of my best work has gotten done in this way. The way we communicate nonverbally speaks volumes about how we really feel and, for this reason, is well worth the extra time these types of efforts may take. Nonverbal codes of communicating are completely lost during remote communication, and that reason, more than any other, is the main argument for communicating directly whenever possible. (For details on nonverbal communication, see Chapter 11.)

DETERMINE NEEDS

While the Internet is an unsurpassed venue for gathering information, that information tends to be superficial. Even organizations that claim to be able to amass personal information about customers such as their financial situations, addresses, and other similar information are still operating on a very surface level. This information is certainly useful for the purposes of qualifying and categorizing customers, but it can never supplant personal contact. As I mentioned in the preceding section, personal contact is how we are able to build the relationships that lead to the unearthing of needs no one may have considered before. Unfortunately, powerful market forces have led us to believe that remote communication can replace direct communication. As a result, we have become so dependent on it that we have forgotten just how powerful face-to-face or at least voice-to-voice communicating can be. In fact, direct communication has emerged as a differentiator. People who practice it stand apart from the group. Remote communication may be easier in the short run. After all, who doesn't fantasize about making a living from the comfort of one's own desk? In the long term, however, the benefits of direct communication are tangible and real.

I am much more interested in making life easier for my clients than for myself. I consider it to be one of my primary responsibilities. In part, this means making myself available and constantly conceiving of creative ways to help and to understand them. Since so much of my preparation involves questioning, I continue to fine-tune this painstaking art. And after asking a question, I must then step back and listen to the answer. Clients are often at a loss to describe what they really need. Many salespeople like myself find this frustrating, and I hear a lot of griping about it. I guess these businesspeople think that their clients already should *know* what they want *before* they call someone in to supply the product or service. But I believe that it is my job, as the expert in the field, to ask the kinds of questions that will uncover the issues the client may be having trouble articulating. (There is much more on questions in Chapter 10). My most important question—and the one that I begin with—goes something like this:

> What would you like to be different as a result of obtaining this product/service?

It also can be

> What changes do you expect to see if you buy and implement this product/ service?

This type of question gets to right to the heart of the matter and sets the stage for further questions that should narrow the focus and fine-tune what eventually will become the final product or service.

Of course, sometimes we do not have the luxury of time to spend thinking, strategizing, planning, and questioning. We need to assess client or customer needs on the spot. This is most true of retail businesses such as stores, where customers approach and enter without warning. It requires a very special skill set to deal with strangers, many of whom you may never see again. Still, all businesses, including stores, have at their core a need for repeat business. In this case, therefore, the proprietor must behave as if every customer who enters will be coming back in the future and must impress the importance of that need on employees. Unfortunately, as most of us know, it doesn't always work that way. The following two stories are instructive.

The "Maine" Message

Every year my family and I go to Maine for vacation. We love it there. It's very informal, not very crowded, and of course, loaded with natural beauty that residents of the state take tremendous pride in. It also has great seafood at great prices. During a visit to the local supermarket, my husband decided to stop by the fish counter to check out lobster prices. Ahead of him was a woman who wanted some salmon. Prices were marked in two places: on flags planted next to the fish on ice and on a blackboard. The price for the salmon on ice said $4.99 a pound, but the blackboard said $3.99 a pound. Guess what price the customer latched on to? After the customer made it clear to the counter person that she expected him to sell it to her for the lower price, the price on the blackboard, he stated that $3.99 a pound was yesterday's price, which had been left accidentally on the blackboard and was no longer valid. Today's price was posted in the case next to the salmon, $4.99 a pound. Well, the customer dug her heels in and insisted on the lower price. The counter person was just as stubborn, asserting that today's price was a dollar higher, and he wasn't going to budge. After a couple of minutes of back and forth, the counter person took control by erasing the blackboard. It was as if the $3.99 price had never existed. The woman's mouth dropped open and she stormed off, *sans* salmon.

When my husband told me this story, we had a good laugh, but we also discussed why the counter person didn't just sell the salmon to that woman for yesterday's price and *then* erase the board. That is certainly what the store where I regularly shop for food would have done. It would have satisfied the customer's need to pay the lowest advertised price, and while it may have cost the market a dollar or two, it would have been more than made up for in good will and a repeat customer.

Another time in Maine I was shopping in a tourist area. At the time, Beanie Babies were very popular, and my younger daughter derived hours of pleasure playing with them. She saw one that she liked in one store for sale at $6.99 and then a few doors down the street the same Beanie for $7.99. Feeling lazy and not wanting to backtrack, I figured I'd appeal to the store clerk by telling her that I had seen the exact same toy in the other store for a dollar less. I was confident that she'd match the price. I was wrong. I approached the counter, laid my $20 bill down, and told her my plan. She responded, in a very loud voice, *"We don't care!"* I'll tell you, it's rare that I become speechless, but this was one of those times. Fortunately, it only lasted for a few seconds, at which point I picked up my money and walked out, energetically strode over to the previous store, and got the cheaper toy. Are you getting the picture here?

Now I should mention that I actually think each of these store salespeople had the right to sell their wares at the prices they had set. But there were alternatives to the ways they handled the situations. In the food market, instead of being stubborn and arguing with the customer about the price, the counter person could have politely explained to the customer that there had been an error and that he was very sorry about the misunderstanding (see Chapter 16 for more on apologizing and explaining). And if he had absolutely no discretion regarding selling it at the lower price, he could have said that if he sold it to her at that price, it would come out of his pocket. The woman selling the Beanie Baby could've politely said that her store's policy was not to compete on price with neighboring retailers, although she could certainly understand if I wanted to return to the other store instead of purchasing it at hers. And was there anything else she could show me that I might want to buy?

As I said earlier, I love Maine and have met some lovely people there. But it is telling that Maine ranks 36 out of 50 in per-capita income in the United States in a region that is home to the states that rank 1, 2, and 3. The moral to these stories is that it would've been a better choice in each case to give the customers what they needed. The short-term loss of money would have been worth the long-term good will that was created.

Being able to asses clients' or customers' needs, sometimes as a result of lengthy and careful probing and questioning, sometimes at the spur of the moment, can make the difference in whether business gets done and money changes hands. As Jack Mitchell, CEO of Mitchells/Richards, a high-end retailer, and author of the best-selling book, *Hug Your Customers: The Proven Way to Personalize Sales and Achieve Astounding Results,* notes: ". . . in the new business landscape, it's no longer enough to have satisfied [or even very satisfied] customers. They must be extremely satisfied."[2] Be sensitive to people's moods. If there is an error or confusing information, give customers the benefit of the doubt. It'll pay big dividends in the long run.

Whenever possible, communicate in person; second best is communicating by phone. (You will hear me saying this throughout this book.) However, with people working from far-flung places or keeping far-flung hours, online communication, even though entirely devoid of nonverbal communication, is acceptable, but *only* under such circumstances. Regardless of the way you get information, the point is to learn as much as possible about the people you will be coming into contact with so that you can target their needs accurately.

Oh, and I still love Maine and absolutely recommend it as a vacation destination. It really is a beautiful place filled with many wonderful people who *will* take your needs to heart.

Ruth's Truths for Chapter 5

Ruth's truth 22: Learn as much as possible before embarking on a communication.

Ruth's truth 23: The Internet is a good source of surface information.

Ruth's truth 24: Remote communication is a good adjunct but not a substitute for direct communication.

Ruth's truth 25: It is the job of the supplier of services or products to uncover client needs.

Ruth's truth 26: To get to the heart of a client's needs, ask the question, "What would you like to be different . . . ?"

Ruth's truth 27: Sometimes you have to assess client needs on the spot, so be prepared for this possibility.

Your Place or Mine? Know the Venue

At the same time we are learning about our customers and clientele, the *encountered,* we need to be aware of the communication landscape, the *encounter.* Lest I sound like a control freak (which people who know me well might argue that I am), I have found that if given a choice, bringing people into your own communication sphere, on your own turf, is worth the effort. The logic is to *maintain control.* The only two aspects we have control over are the *encounterer* and to a lesser but significant extent the *encounter.*

LET ME ENTERTAIN YOU

As with all communication, controlling the encounter requires a lot of effort. One thing I always recommend to clients is that whenever possible, important communications should be conducted on their own turf. There is a great deal to be said for the home field advantage. Inviting people to your office or, if circumstances allow, to your home confers a great advantage. I am a huge fan of the dinner party. Having people to your home for dinner continues to be a terrific way to build relationships in a situation where you have ultimate control over the venue. Let's look at some of the reasons such an event is so worthwhile:

- Your home is unquestionably your turf and communicates a great deal about who you are.[1]
- Preparing a dinner party takes tremendous organizational skills.

- The host controls the conversation.
- Delicious, well-presented food makes people feel happy; happy people are more open.
- A successful dinner party will be remembered and appreciated, spawning long-lasting good feelings.

Aside from inviting guests to my home, I'm a big fan of doing business over meals in restaurants and other establishments. Possibilities include lunch, dinner, drinks and hors d'oeuvres, and coffee and dessert. There is also my favorite, breakfast. Many people don't think about breakfast as appropriate for business dining, but it's got a lot going for it for the following reasons:

- Conflicts and cancellations are far fewer; people are not coming from their workplaces, so last-minute work interruptions are not nearly as likely to arise.
- People are more alert, and their moods are not yet influenced by their day's happenings.
- Restaurants are not as crowded, and the atmosphere is much less frenetic than at other times.
- There is little chance that alcohol will be served, thus eliminating a potential complication.

One of the best places to have breakfast is a hotel restaurant. Hotel dining rooms specialize in this meal, and many are oriented specifically to business customers. They also open at an early hour, unlike many restaurants. The tables are atypically large and not placed too closely together, and the chairs are often upholstered for comfort. The noise level tends to be low. The only downside is that they tend to be more expensive than other types of restaurants. Still, I highly recommend hotels for business breakfasts.

EXPLORE THE SURROUNDINGS

Whenever I have to give a presentation or schedule a meeting with a new client, I make an attempt to investigate the venue. If it is to take place at a client location and it is within a reasonable distance, I make it a point to see the actual room. Another tactic is to go to the offices of clients I plan to meet with a few days in advance of our appointment. A strategy I use is to call and ask if it would be possible for me to obtain company information such as an annual report or company brochure or press kit and offer to stop by and pick it up. This tactic also serves the purpose of helping to prepare for the meeting with written information. For example, annual reports often contain photographs of the corporate leaders, employees, and the offices. From the logo you can gain a sense of the sophistication and sensibilities of the company. Many times there will be a mission statement that can enlighten you to the corporate philosophy. While it's true that you can get a lot of this information these days by logging on to a company's Web site, by actually being at an office and observing the people going about their business, you can pick up a lot of additional information, such as the dress code, and gain ideas about the level of formality of the organization. I also can glean information from the way the office is decorated, such as the importance the company puts on its public face and how much money it spends on such things.

When it is not possible to explore the location in person, it has to be done long distance. About a year ago I was asked to give a presentation at a conference in San Antonio, Texas, where I had never been. San Antonio, I ultimately found, is a great city, home of the Alamo and full of friendly, helpful people. About a month before the conference, I called the hotel where the conference was being held and asked to be connected with the media services department. I spoke to Joseph, who had been charged with catering to the audio/visual needs of conference speakers. I was very organized, knew just what I needed, and was prepared with questions for Joseph. He was very accommodating and did a good job of describing the layout of the room in which I would be speaking, the facilities, and any pitfalls I might encounter. We had two or three conversations prior to the conference. I sent Joseph a checklist of equipment I would need. I had booked my flight so that it would arrive early enough that I would have plenty of time before my presentation to meet with Joseph and have him show me the room and locations of all the various plugs, outlets, and switches. I also knew that I would not be the only speaker assigned to that room during the three days of the conference, so I wanted to have some time in the room when no one else needed it. All this preparation and attention to detail paid off nicely; on meeting for the first time, Joseph and I felt like we already knew each other. The presentation went very smoothly, and I gained some excellent new clients. Had I lived nearby, I certainly would have made it a point to go to the hotel in advance and check things out. However, as I found out, this also can be done from afar. (After the conference, I sent a letter to the hotel manager praising Joseph.)

It's always a good idea to explore the surroundings to the best of your ability. The more control you have over the environment, the more comfortable you'll be and be able to make others. Also, mistakes and chance events, those pesky but inevitable little glitches that turn up in the most carefully planned situations, are much less likely to derail you. Again, this requires time to organize and plan but will show positive results in terms of increased esteem. Your audience will view you as having things very much under control. People who have things under control are people clients want to do business with. And in case you're thinking that all this is starting to sound a bit contrived, I urge you to look up the word *contrivance*. You'll see it defined as an "ingenious plan." This type of behavior forecasts your competence to clients who are looking for *their* next ingenious plan.

Ruth's Truths for Chapter 6

Ruth's truth 28: Whenever possible, important communication should be conducted on your own turf, whether it be your office, home, or another location of your choosing.

Ruth's truth 29: Meals are excellent venues for doing business.

Ruth's truth 30: Dinner parties are good ways to demonstrate organizational skills and build business relationships.

Ruth's truth 31: Breakfast is a little used but effective business meal.

Ruth's truth 32: When meeting on foreign turf, try to explore it first; directly is best, but remotely is fine if there is no other practical choice.

Seize the Moment

Now let's turn our attention to the myriad opportunities that exist to win people over and that are presented to us each and every day. There are so many that it's a wonder we don't seize more of them. Recognizing opportunities to make contact and build relationships is an important and obvious first step. So where might these opportunities lie? At work, the following are openings:

- Internal meetings
- External meetings
- Speeches and presentations
- Galas and fundraisers
- Phone conversations
- Sales calls
- Informal meals
- Formal meals
- Association get-togethers
- Conventions and conferences
- Workshops and seminars
- Office kitchens and public spaces
- Private offices
- Elevators
- Travel
- Business social events

If you do not work in a business environment, you may be busy volunteering in schools or hospitals or lending your expertise and energy to nonprofit or civic organizations. Opportunities are numerous here too:

- Board meetings
- Committee meetings
- Exercise groups
- Coffee shop
- Business dinners of spouse
- Holiday parties
- Galas and fundraisers
- Phone conversations
- Shopping
- Picking kids up from school
- Playground
- Home/school organizations
- School events

If you are a spouse who does not have another job outside the home, networking on behalf of your husband or wife is de rigueur. Many spouses (usually wives) have, through neighborhood networking, secured opportunities for their partners that would have gone to someone else had they not been alert and seized the moment. In fact, whether they are working outside the home or not, spouses always should be looking out for each other and gathering information that could be helpful. I know I always have an ear trained for information that may help my husband, and I have been known to approach relative strangers directly when I sense an opening. The thing is that you never know when one of these opportunities is going to present itself, so you need to be ready to pounce.

DEVELOP YOUR INTRODUCTORY PITCH

Finally, we have a chance to get into some of the details that apply to the *encounterer,* the last part of the equation that I introduced in Chapter 5. How often are you required to introduce and tell people about yourself? How often is what you say less than optimal? This used to be my experience. I never seemed to be able to spit out everything I wanted to say about who I was and what I did in the heat of the moment. For some reason, I thought it should be spontaneous, the words spilling over my lips in a cascade of beautifully articulated phrases and sentences, all grammatically perfect. I envied people who could do this well. Then I learned their secret: They had taken the time to sit down and create an introductory pitch.

An introductory pitch should be short and to the point. It should tell people what you do and what's in it for them. The following is an introduction I use when I expect to be meeting potential corporate clients:

> My company trains corporate executives in communication and presentation skills. We provide workshops and seminars and specialize in helping very senior executives to leverage high-stakes communication opportunities such as keynotes, road shows, and media contact.

Now, let's analyze the structure of this pitch:

> *Sentence 1: My company trains corporate executives in communication and presentation skills.* This sentence states exactly what my company does.
>
> *Sentence 2, part 1: We provide workshops and seminars . . .* This first part of the sentence describes a general service to a more mass audience.
>
> *Sentence 2, part 2: . . . and specialize in helping very senior executives to leverage high-stakes communication opportunities . . .* This part describes a specialty area that is unique. This is a classic sales tool known as a unique selling proposition (USP) first identified and coined by the great adman Ted Bates.
>
> *Sentence 2, part 3: . . . such as keynotes, road shows, and media contact.* Here I list some of the venues where the services are provided. This usually generates a good deal of interest.

Most important, the pitch is very concise and efficient. It's packed with information, uses very few words, and takes just a moment to deliver. It provokes questions and encourages conversation. This is known as a *hook.* A hook grabs attention and practically begs for further inquiry on the part of the listener.

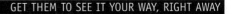
Because one pitch does not fit every situation, I adjust it as necessary to accommodate other listeners. For example, to a group where I believe I would meet potential coaching clients, I would say the following:

> My company provides training in communication and presentation skills. We help people to become more effective communicators so that they can have a bigger impact in their professional and personal lives.

In my personal life, when I am wearing my "mommy" hat and volunteering in one of my children's schools, I say

> Hi, I'm [name of my child]'s mom.

Nothing more is needed because from there the other person introduces herself, and the conversation naturally turns to matters of family, children, and school. This almost always leads to opportunities to engage in conversations about work and/or my interests. Perhaps that will be the end of it; not all conversations must or should generate leads. But perhaps. . . . Well, by now you may recognize that I am ever the optimist. The bottom line is that opportunities not seized are opportunities lost.

Use the following format to write out some introductory pitches that could work for you. Remember that the format is only a guide and should be adapted as you make it your own. The key is to be concise and efficient by packing a lot of information into relatively few words. Below is a template for creating your own introductory pitches.

Create Your Introductory Pitches

Audience 1 (Who are they?)_____

Introductory Pitch A

Sentence 1 (Give a brief description of the primary service or product of you or your company.) _____

_____

_____

Sentence 2, part 1 (Describe how the services/products are delivered.)

_____

_____

Sentence 2, part 2 (Describe a unique niche, a USP.) _____

_____

_____

Sentence 2, part 3 (List two or three examples of areas in which your services/products are used.) _____

_____

_____

Audience 2 (Who are they?)_____

Introductory Pitch B

Sentence 1 (Give a brief description of the primary service or product of you or your company.) _____

_____

_____

Sentence 2, part 1 (Describe how the services/products are delivered.)

_____

_____

Sentence 2, part 2 (Describe a unique niche, a USP.) _____

_____

_____

Sentence 2, part 3 (List two or three examples of areas in which your services/products are used.) _____

_____

_____

Audience 3 (Who are they?)_____

Introductory Pitch C

Sentence 1 (Give a brief description of the primary service or product of you or your company.) _____

_____

_____

> *Sentence 2, part 1* (Describe how the services/products are delivered.)
> _____
> _____
> _____
>
> *Sentence 2, part 2* (Describe a unique niche, a USP.) _____
> _____
> _____
>
> *Sentence 2, part 3* (List two or three examples of areas in which your services/products are used.) _____
> _____
> _____

Once you've written your introductory pitch(es), it's time to go out and practice. As a preliminary exercise, you might want to record and play them back or get feedback from friends or family. But there are absolutely no prohibitions about just jumping right in and using your new pitch the next time you have an opportunity.

DETERMINE YOUR MAIN MESSAGE

To get off on the right foot communicating, you need a clearly defined objective and a main message. The objective addresses the general question, "Why am I communicating?" The main message offers a point of view. The main message should be used as a benchmark. By the time you are finished communicating, you should be able to look at that main message and know whether you have accomplished the objective that describes it.

We must be careful not to confuse meeting our objective with whether or not people follow the advice or suggestions made in the main message. For example, if we look at objective 3 on the next page, "Make strategy recommendations," it doesn't mean that you've failed if the listeners do not follow your recommendation. The only benchmark you have to meet is whether you accomplished your objective. The following table presents seven objectives that I believe cover most, if not all, aspects of communication along with some business and personal examples of main messages that fit the objectives.

OBJECTIVE	MAIN MESSAGE
1. Share information	*Work example:* "I have completed the report and would like to tell you about the results."
	Personal example: "I got some information on some new cars."
2. Sell an idea	*Work example:* "We should consider purchasing a new system."
	Personal example: "I think we should go on a vacation to a national park this summer."
3. Make strategy recommendations	*Work example:* "Based on my research, I think it makes sense to enter this new business area."
	Personal example: "If we take the interstate, we can avoid getting too close to the city at rush hour."
4. Recommend alternatives	*Work example:* "In order to meet our goals going forward, I think we ought to change our management structure."
	Personal example: "We could have the party at home instead of out to save some money."
5. Identify existing or potential problems	*Work example:* "We've identified two problems with the Midwest group."
	Personal example: "The car is making a funny noise, so I think I'd better take it in."
6. Communicate news—good or bad	*Work example:* "Our fourth-quarter results are up (or down) 8 percent."
	Personal example: "Guess what? Peg and Bob are getting married!"
7. Teach a skill	*Work example:* "Today we are going to give you some tools and techniques designed to help you negotiate deals."
	Personal example: "When you cook pancakes, you have to make sure you flip them before they burn."

The primary advantage to defining your objective is that it *saves time.* In addition, it helps you to organize quickly. It also forces you to plan, focuses and narrows your research, and helps you to limit your audience. Having something simple at your fingertips tends to encourage you to get going and not procrastinate.

USE THE *SALES* TOOL FOR FOOLPROOF ORGANIZING

Now that you've got something you want to talk about, it's time to organize your thoughts. With everyone's time at a premium, it's important to be concise and systematic about what you want to say. No one likes to listen to rambling or verbose speech. You need to be efficient. To help my clients and myself with this, I developed a tool called *SALES:*

> *S* tate your main message.
> *A* dd key points.
> *L* ist benefits.
> *E* xamples, stories, and vignettes.
> *S* ummarize and specify next steps.

SALES works in every situation outlined in this chapter and in most situations mentioned in this book. It is especially effective when you're put on the spot, when you're on the phone, and when you are sending or responding to e-mails. Using *SALES* has helped my clients and me stay focused and organized. It should take no more than one minute to deliver a message formatted with this tool. *SALES* also reminds us why we're communicating (sell, persuade, win over). Being put on the spot can be very trying, and the pressure to perform or respond well is fairly high. Still, there's no reason to buckle. Take a breath, and think *SALES.* I guarantee that it will help you to think calmly, rationally, and concisely. It will help you to position and support your ideas. (One further tip: If you are really pressed for time, think consonants only: *S-L-S.*)

Following is an example of a response using *SALES* that a client of mine used when he was put on the spot by the chairman of his company who wanted a quick status report on a project my client was working on:

State your main message: "The project has been going relatively smoothly, with only a few glitches that you've been made aware of. We're on schedule."

Add key points: "We'll be completing phase 1 this weekend, testing the system and working out any bugs. Anne and Rob are both coming in, along with a couple of people they've tapped, so we've got the necessary personnel to see this phase through."

List benefits: "Once this is done, we will have cleared a major hurdle. Phases 2 and 3 pretty much repeat many of the same steps, and that playbook will have been written. The other good thing is that by the time all is said and done, Anne and Rob will be up to speed on the project and ready to take it to the other locations and manage the process there."

Examples, stories, vignettes: "As you know, I worked on a similar project at my last company. I learned a lot from that experience. For example, one pitfall was that we didn't leave enough time to train the employees before the system went up. The training program we've designed for this project is excellent and actually has had the additional effect of firing up the staff—they're raring to go."

Summarize and specify next steps: "So we're on track with phase 1, finishing it this weekend. After testing, we'll be moving on to the next stages, which are scheduled to go up in 6 and 12 weeks, respectively. Then we'll be ready to take it online."

As you may have guessed, the project was a major systems overhaul that, had it not gone smoothly, would have virtually shut down operations at the company. There was a lot riding on its success. Keeping higher-ups informed is a good way to get them to see things your way—and to be left alone to do important work.

SALES Sample Scenarios

Following are a few cumulative scenarios that demonstrate how a *SALES* "pitch" can be built and delivered quickly.

*S*tate Your Main Message

- *Ask yourself why make the call?*
  S: "I'm calling to get your input on the candidates for training."
- *Ask yourself why write the e-mail?*
  S: "I've attached a proposal for the work that you requested."
- *Ask yourself why go to the event?*
  S: "I'm very interested in hearing the speaker."
- *Ask yourself why call the meeting?*
  S: "We need to review the progress of the project to see where things stand."
- *Ask yourself why make the appointment?*
  S: "I'd like to let you know about some of the work I've been doing for the agency."

  Know what you want.

*A*dd Key Points

- *During the phone call:*
  S: "I'm calling to get your input on the candidates for training."
  A: "They seem to have a lot in common, and I plan to speak to each of them before the training begins."
- *In the e-mail:*
  S: "I've attached a proposal for the work that you requested."
  A: "It contains all the information you requested, including a time frame for roll-out and costs."
- *At the event:*
  S: "I'm very interested in hearing the speaker."
  A: "He wrote a book that I read recently, and I think he's got a lot of insights into the market in these difficult economic times. I'm particularly interested in what he has to say about interest rates."
- *During the meeting:*
  S: "We need to review the progress of the project to see where things stand."
  A: "Right now, things seem to be on track, but I'm concerned about certain costs, particularly from the builder. I don't want things to spiral out of control."

- *While making the appointment:*
  S: "I'd like to let you know about some of the work I've been doing for the agency."
  A: "I've just finished the campaign for the new product and have begun to write copy for the antidrug campaign we're doing pro bono. I'd like to bring both of them by and get your feedback."

*L*ist Benefits

- *During the phone call:*
  S: "I'm calling to get your input on the candidates for training."
  A: "They seem to have a lot in common, and I plan to speak to each of them before the training begins."
  L: "Information from both sources will help me to better target the content."
- *In the e-mail:*
  S: "I've attached a proposal for the work that you requested."
  A: "It contains all the information you requested, including a time frame for roll-out and costs."
  L: "I've created a type of cafeteria plan so that you can choose one that suits you best. The inherent flexibility is a win for everyone."
- *At the event:*
  S: "I'm very interested in hearing the speaker."
  A: "He wrote a book that I read recently, and I think he's got a lot of insights into the market in these difficult economic times. I'm particularly interested in what he has to say about interest rates."
  L: "I always find myself being more motivated after hearing speakers like this one, and I end up getting a lot of work done."
- *During the meeting:*
  S: "We need to review the progress of the project to see where things stand."
  A: "Right now, things seem to be on track, but I'm concerned about certain costs, particularly from the builder. I don't want things to spiral out of control."
  L: "If we ask some questions now, we have a much better chance of avoiding problems later."
- *While making the appointment:*
  S: "I'd like to let you know about some of the work I've been doing for the agency."

A: "I've just finished the campaign for the new product and have begun to write copy for the antidrug campaign we're doing pro bono. I'd like to bring both of them by and get your feedback."

L: "This way you can see what I've been doing so that we can be sure that I'm headed in the right direction. Also, I could really use another set of eyes."

*E*xamples, Stories, and Vignettes

- *During the phone call:*

  S: "I'm calling to get your input on the candidates for training."

  A: "They seem to have a lot in common, and I plan to speak to each of them before the training begins."

  L: "Information from both sources will help me to better target the content."

  E: "The last time I did this for you, I was not as prepared as I wanted to be. Although the participants benefited, I thought they could've gotten more."

- *In the e-mail:*

  S: "I've attached a proposal for the work that you requested."

  A: "It contains all the information you requested, including a time frame for roll-out and costs."

  L: "I've created a type of cafeteria plan so that you can choose one that suits you best. The inherent flexibility is a win for everyone."

  E: "We haven't done it like this before, but a colleague of mine has, and it was very successful. Also, there was a study done on this type of setup that showed that it is a good fit for your type of business."

- *At the event:*

  S: "I'm very interested in hearing the speaker."

  A: "He wrote a book that I read recently, and I think he's got a lot of insights into the market in these difficult economic times. I'm particularly interested in what he has to say about interest rates."

L: "I always find myself being more motivated after hearing speakers like this one, and I end up getting a lot of work done."

E: "I was at a convention where I heard a similar speaker. After listening to her, I returned to my office and, by using one of her techniques, got one of my biggest accounts yet."

- *During the meeting:*

  S: "We need to review the progress of the project to see where things stand."

  A: "Right now, things seem to be on track, but I'm concerned about certain costs, particularly from the builder. I don't want things to spiral out of control."

  L: "If we ask some questions now, we have a much better chance of avoiding problems later."

  E: "On the last project, we were very careful—too careful perhaps—but the result was good. But you may recall that on the project we undertook in 2000, costs did get out of hand. We learned from that."

- *While making the appointment:*

  S: "I'd like to let you know about some of the work I've been doing for the agency."

  A: "I've just finished the campaign for the new product and have begun to write copy for the antidrug campaign we're doing pro bono. I'd like to bring both of them by and get your feedback."

  L: "This way you can see what I've been doing so that we can be sure I'm headed in the right direction. Also, I could really use another set of eyes."

  E: "When we got together last quarter, it was very helpful to have your input. You may remember that after that meeting I changed direction, and we ended up winning more business."

Summarize and Specify Next Steps

- *During the phone call:*

  S: "I'm calling to get your input on the candidates for training."

  A: "They seem to have a lot in common, and I plan to speak to each of them before the training begins."

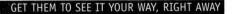

L: "Information from both sources will help me to better target the content."

E: "The last time I did this for you, I was not as prepared as I wanted to be. Although the participants benefited, I thought they could've gotten more."

S: "So, when it's convenient for you, I'd like to schedule some time to discuss it. Can we schedule a time now?"

- *In the e-mail:*

  S: "I've attached a proposal for the work that you requested."

  A: "It contains all the information you requested, including a time frame for roll-out and costs."

  L: "I've created a type of cafeteria plan so that you can choose one that suits you best. The inherent flexibility is a win for everyone."

  E: "We haven't done it like this before, but a colleague of mine has, and it was very successful. Also, there was a study done on this type of setup that showed that it is a good fit for your type of business."

  S: "You'll need some time to review the proposal. I'm available if you have any questions or need clarification. Would it be all right for me to follow-up next week, say, on Tuesday?"

- *At the event:*

  S: "I'm very interested in hearing the speaker."

  A: "He wrote a book that I read recently, and I think he's got a lot of insights into the market in these difficult economic times. I'm particularly interested in what he has to say about interest rates."

  L: "I always find myself being more motivated after hearing speakers like this one, and I end up getting a lot of work done."

  E: "I was at a convention where I heard a similar speaker. After listening to her, I returned to my office and, by using one of her techniques, got one of my biggest accounts yet."

  S: "So, the way I look at it, it's a cheap way to keep moving forward and get some great new ideas. Oh, looks like things are about to get started. Let's grab a seat."

- *During the meeting:*
    S: "We need to review the progress of the project to see where things stand."
    A: "Right now, things seem to be on track, but I'm concerned about certain costs, particularly from the builder. I don't want things to spiral out of control."
    L: "If we ask some questions now, we have a much better chance of avoiding problems later."
    E: "On the last project, we were very careful—too careful per-haps—but the result was good. But you may recall that on the project we undertook in 2000, costs did get out of hand. We learned from that."
    S: "E-mail me any questions you have about it by tomorrow after-noon. Then I'll call the contractor and try to get some answers. I'll get back to you as soon as I have something. Then we may have to meet again."
- *While making the appointment:*
    S: "I'd like to let you know about some of the work I've been doing for the agency."
    A: "I've just finished the campaign for the new product and have begun to write copy for the antidrug campaign we're doing pro bono. I'd like to bring both of them by and get your feedback."
    L: "This way you can see what I've been doing so that we can be sure I'm headed in the right direction. Also, I could really use another set of eyes."
    E: "When we got together last quarter, it was very helpful to have your input. You may remember that after that meeting I changed direction, and we ended up winning more business."
    S: "I was thinking that perhaps we could meet at the end of the day next Wednesday or Friday. I'm flexible, so please let me know."

Taking a systematic approach makes *SALES* an easy and pain-free way to communicate thoughts and turn them into actions. Use the follow-ing form to organize your communications with *SALES*.

SALES Organization Chart

*S*tate Your Main Message

_____

_____

_____

_____

*A*dd Key Points

1. _____

2. _____

3. _____

4. _____

*L*ist the Benefits

1. _____

2. _____

3. _____

4. _____

*E*xamples, Stories, and Vignettes

_____

_____

_____

_____

*S*ummarize and Specify Next Steps

_____

_____

_____

_____

SALES is also a terrific tool to use for leaving voice mail and sending e-mail. See Chapter 15 for a discussion and some ideas about how to use this technique in these media.

TELL ME A STORY: MATERIAL TO MAKE YOUR PITCH COME ALIVE

The *E* in SALES is meant to remind us to include examples, stories, and vignettes. Incorporating stories or anecdotes makes an interchange seem real. Stories add the element of authenticity to what otherwise might be a recitation of dry data. Stories show that there are real-life applications to accompany the data. Stories make material of any kind sing.

When Hayley came to me, she had been growing increasingly frustrated with her lack of success in keeping people's attention during the many pitches and presentations she had to make as a regional sales manager for a medical supply company. While she once had been able to count on the exclusivity and uniqueness of her company's products, the competition had been gaining ground, and she felt that she needed something more to persuade clients to remain with her and her company's products.

I asked Hayley to do some role practice with me, pretending that I was a client with whom she was communicating. Her initial movements and speech were very comfortable. She came across as confident and personable. She also was up on current events that were relevant to her clients' businesses. I could see how she had been so successful. So far, so good. After some small talk, Hayley launched into her presentation. She whipped out her laptop, set it down at a place on the table where she and I (in the role of "client") could sit and view it together, booted it up, and loaded her PowerPoint presentation. She had loads of images and data and took us through about 25 slides, pointing out the most germane information. She was very focused and did not digress. All this took a total of about 30 minutes.

When she finished, I told her that although she was incredibly well prepared and knowledgeable about the market, the pitch lost steam once she got started with the PowerPoint. The personal strengths that she brought to the relationship had gotten buried under layers of mind-numbing data depicted in color-coded charts, graphs, and animation. The presentation software, I believed, placed a barrier between her and her client. In addition, numbers, facts, and figures usually are too dry to be spoken of without other rhetorical devices that serve to add warmth and spice to the communication. If she had been using *SALES* to help organize and plan the interaction, she would have seen the spot where it makes sense to add stories and vignettes. Finally, I told her that if I had actually been her client and knew what I was in store for, I would be inclined to ask her to send it to me so that I could read it myself rather than spend valuable time having her read it to me.

This was not welcome news. Hayley had been doing her presentations the same way for years, and the approach had always served her well. Furthermore, she asserted that clients expected and wanted this type of presentation. PowerPoint helped to put complex data into easier-to-understand forms.1 I reminded her that she came to me precisely for these reasons: The old ways didn't seem to be working anymore. I also stated that old habits are hard to change and that this can feel risky, causing resistance.

When I asked her how she felt about the first part of actual client conversations that included the greeting and small talk, she replied that it felt good and pointed to a discussion that she had with a client about a cutting-edge development in the field that she had just read about in a trade journal and that the client likely would have seen too. (She would have brought it with her, just in case.) She told me that this part of client conversations was very interactive and brought to light some new thoughts on both her and her clients' parts. I pointed out that the trade journal article was a story and that more stories would enliven her pitch.

Then the real barrier was exposed: Hayley didn't know where to find stories. It is a typical problem that many of my clients encounter. When I told her that stories are found everywhere, she was heartened. This book, for example, is peppered with stories, including this one. Some writers call them cases or case studies. Whatever they are called, their purpose is to illustrate a point, make that point real, and provide solutions to problems. Stories are available from the following sources:

- Clients
- Colleagues
- Suppliers

- Family
- Friends
- Reading material of all kinds
- Television, radio, and other broadcast media
- The Internet

All the stories I use—in this book, in my interpersonal communications, and in my public speaking as well—stem from one of the preceding sources. It's important to know how to weave a story into discourse. In Chapter 8, I discuss at length the benefits of reading and the discipline required to clip and retain material that you find interesting and that you may be able to use. But again, although reading is one of the richest hunting grounds for material, there are others.

Working a story into a sales pitch or conversation can be handled in a variety of ways:

- I saw an article in the paper yesterday that said. . . .
- [*Name of a well-known person*] contends that. . . .
- I have another client who tried that product and had some difficulties making it operational. . . .
- My friend Alyssa had a funny thing happen to her the other day. . . .
- When I was president of the other nonprofit group. . . .
- I was at a networking event last Friday and was talking to [*name of colleague*], who said. . . .
- I just finished [*name of a relevant author*]'s latest book. Her premise is that. . . .
- How many people have seen the movie [*title of movie*]? Well, those who have seen it may remember the scene where. . . .
- My friend Simon, who is an investment banker, was facing a particularly difficult set of circumstances. . . .
- I was in the market for some new [*whatever*]. When I began my search, I was astonished at the number of choices. I didn't know which way to turn. So I. . . .
- This happened to me one time [*recount the story*]. . . .
- When I first started in this line of work. . . .
- I have a great story for you. . . .

- I just heard a really funny story. . . .
- I'd like to tell you a story about something that happened. . . .

Choosing the right story to fit the occasion can be challenging. The best stories are personal; they stem directly from your own experiences—you read something, you heard something, you saw something, you experienced something. The next best are stories that someone else told you. The third choice would be stories from a third-party source, such as something you read or saw on TV or online. There are also tons of reference books that contain stories and jokes. They're often referred to as "speakers' treasuries." I personally find it very difficult to harvest appropriate material from these sources. Most of the material was written for someone else or for a specific occasion and doesn't translate well. But they are categorized to help you to discriminate among the entries, and since you can adapt the stories to your own needs, it pays to have a few of these books on hand for reference. The Internet also has some terrific sites for quotations. The bottom line is that the more resources you have, the more successful you'll be at finding good stuff to spice up your communication.

Take care to not fabricate stories. Be mindful of the fact that one of the main considerations for using a story is that it adds a grain of truth to your communication. Phony or concocted stories risk creating the opposite effect—skepticism and doubt. People have a sixth sense when stories do not have a ring of truth. Mistrust can result, and really, what can be worse?

But—and pay attention here—you can manipulate your true stories to make them fit your occasion. For example, perhaps you have a great story that happened a couple of years ago but is still relevant today. Instead of saying, "A couple of years ago when I was on my way into the city by train, . . ." you can say, "I was on my way into the city by train. . . ." You can change names, locations, and other details that would not derail the story (and there are circumstances where you must do that to protect people's privacy). For example, there is a story I tell of being on a plane where a seatmate was rehearsing for a presentation she was on her way to do. This particular incident happened several years ago; however, I see replays of it quite often. Thus, when I tell the story, I don't mention that it happed a few years ago. Instead, I tell it in a way that the audience comes to its own conclusion about when it happened. It so happens that audience members often conclude that it happened recently.

Whatever source you choose, a well-crafted story will motivate, communicate, and teach. Start collecting them now. Here, I'll start you off: "I just read a great book by Ruth Sherman called *Get Them to See It Your Way, Right Away.* In it she says. . . ."

TRANSITIONS AND SEGUES: LINKING POINTS TOGETHER

Moving through communication smoothly requires verbal devices that help you to navigate from section to section. Knowing how to create and use transitions or segues is a vital yet overlooked part of communicating and presenting information. Clients often find themselves stuck on one or two phrases and can't seem to cut loose from them. There are several good reasons to employ transitions in your communications. Transitions

- Lead from one idea to another
- Link points that otherwise might seem tangential
- Provide internal summaries to help listeners know where they are
- Help the communicator to maintain control and guide the direction of the communication
- Get listeners' attention

Following are some techniques to facilitate transitions:

- Write out linking sentences or phrases.
- For long points that contain much detail, try summarizing those points with each transition. These are called *internal summaries.* They are like road maps for the audience; they tell audience members where they have been and where they will be going.
- Physically pause or move in a specific way at the time of the transition to alert listeners to the idea that something new is happening.

I have tried to use transitions throughout this book. In fact, after I wrote the first draft, I went on a transition "hunt" just to make sure that I didn't switch my focus without first preparing my readers for both what had just transpired and what was about to happen.

There are many ways to construct a transition or segue, and following are a few that should be easy to keep in mind:

1. "To move on to the next point. . . ."
2. "Point 3 is. . . ."
3. "My last three points covered. . . . My next three will cover. . . ."
4. "Next, we come to. . . ."
5. "The next section will cover. . . ."
6. "Let's turn to the next page. . . ."
7. "Are there any questions so far?" (Pause and look around, answer any questions, or move on to new point.)
8. "If there are no questions. . . ."
9. "Now that we've covered . . ., let's take a look at. . . ."
10. "In addition. . . ."
11. "I'd like to change direction now. . . ."
12. "If I may, I'd like to switch the focus to. . . ."
13. "Turning to. . . ."
14. "Another idea to consider is. . . ."

Internal summaries, mentioned above, are designed to summarize segments of your communication periodically as you move through it. For example:

> So what I've just described is a business area that has grown surprisingly well and to which we may have to add more resources. [*internal summary*] Now I'd like to discuss a couple of areas that are not meeting our expectations. [*transition*]

Some final thoughts about transitions and segues:

- Beware of repeating the same phrase. The most commonly used phrase is "In addition." The next most common is "If we turn to the next page."
- Don't make them too brief.

There are many more. As with all plans for communication, as you think of them, write them down.

TAKE NOTE: USING NOTES TO KEEP ON TRACK

Certain situations lend themselves to having notes handy. Situations such as meetings, phone calls, and certainly presentations of all kinds accommodate notes. However, many people think that notes are an indication of weakness. I must protest!

I was asked to develop and deliver a presentation skills workshop for a group of executives at a global consulting company. During the development phase, Chris, the director who hired me, and I came to the subject of using notes for presentations. He was against it. He felt that using notes showed a lack of knowledge of the topic. He did not want his people using them. I took note (no pun intended) and developed the workshop.

I use notes. I use them all the time, and I use them even if I've done a specific presentation 100 times and know it cold. I like how notes make me feel. They give me security. When I do run into a bit of a mental block, I only have to glance down at my notes to get back on track. How to use notes effectively is a hallmark of my program, so I teach workshop participants about it. I really didn't want to sack this part of my program for the workshop.

During the initial portion of the workshop, Chris sat in. I usually do a lot of speaking during this part. At the break, I asked Chris if he remembered whether I had used notes. He acknowledged that he hadn't noticed but thought that I hadn't. When I told him I had, he smiled and admitted that perhaps notes could be used effectively.

Notes can take many forms. One of the most popular media for notes is the index card. Notes can be written or typed on these cards and used for presentations. I recommend using larger, five by seven inch cards. The good things about using cards are that they are fairly easy to handle, they don't rattle like paper does, and they are stiff and small, requiring only one hand to hold them. TV interviewers use them, and so do speakers and politicians. I treat them as an extension of my hand.

Notes can be on regular paper. This works fine in a meeting setting where you are seated at a table and can look down comfortably. Organize your notes into an outline form. You can jot down ideas that pop into your mind during your discussion.

The most important things to be careful of with notes:

- *Don't pack too much information into too small a space.* Four or five points per index card or per outline segment are enough.
- *Don't write too small or type information in too small a font.* Fourteen-point Arial is a good place to start. There should be plenty of air, so double space. This also leaves room to jot down other, last-minute ideas.
- *Don't write out notes in complete sentences.* This will induce you to read instead of using notes as a trigger.

Using File Folders and Sticky Notes to Organize

Here is a wonderful technique for brainstorming and note gathering using manila file folders and small sticky notes:

1. Try to come up with a main message. Why are you communicating? (If you don't know, it can wait.)
2. Take a manila folder (legal or letter size) and a pad of 1.5- by 2-inch sticky notes.
3. Start brainstorming by writing trigger words or phrases on a sticky note and putting that note anywhere on the folder.
4. Your folder will look something like the top folder on the next page.
5. Once you've exhausted your ideas, start organizing by moving around the sticky notes. Discard ones you don't need.
6. At the top, write down (or stick) the main message.
7. Starting on the left, place a sticky note with a key point. Under that key point, make a column of sticky notes that contain supporting points.
8. Do the same thing in two or three more columns (key point with supporting points under it).
9. Your last column should have your conclusions and close.
10. Your folder will now look something like the bottom folder on the next page.

Don't forget that you can use *SALES* to help crystallize your thoughts.

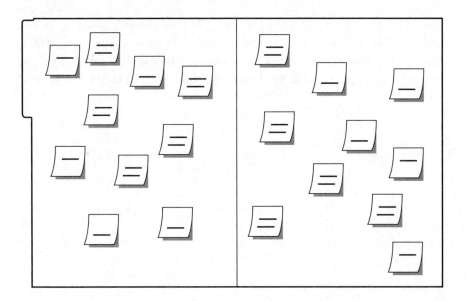

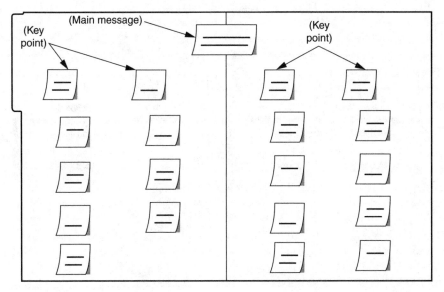

The beauty of the system is that you can move the notes around—there isn't any crossing out and scribbling. In addition, if you get interrupted, you can close the folder and put it away, and everything stays put until you're ready to resume.

There is another method I use to organize thoughts quickly. Some people refer to this form as a *logic tree* because of its shape. I've turned the tree on its side, but it serves the same function. The following figure is an example of how my logic tree might organize a hypothetical situation.

Main message	Key points	Supporting points (2-5 for each key point)	Close/Summary/ Action step
	It will keep people closer to their desks.	Increased productivity. Networking opportunities. Team building opportunities. Social interaction.	
The company should supply lunch to employees.	Morale will be boosted	Employees will feel agency really values them. Agency will get benefit of increased profits. Higher morale = lower turnover	Bottom line: Investment will be worth it
	Requires a significant investment	$100/month per employee, 50 employees = $5000 After subtracting subsidy *y* only $2K Productivity will more than make up the cost.	
	Concerns	Some employees may take advantage. Pulling program will cause resentment.	

Whether you use file folders and sticky notes, logic trees, index cards, or outlines to organize your thoughts, creating notes to use when communicating is crucial to helping you to keep your eyes on the prize. Notes provide the following benefits:

- Notes function as a road map, helping to keep you focused and on track and add to a perception of preparedness.
- Notes serve as a security blanket, providing a safety net should your mind go blank.
- Notes, in proper form, will prevent you from reading verbatim and actually make you look and feel more spontaneous.

As I said at the outset of this section, I always use them, consider them a great aid, and recommend them to all my clients.

Identifying opportunities to communicate, developing an introductory pitch, and practicing its delivery will contribute to the confident impression you want to leave with others. And impressions are made quickly, usually within seconds. Using those precious moments to influence the process takes planning. At the very least, you want to entice people and make them want to know more. Use the tools outlined here, and you'll be on track to deliver.

Ruth's Truths for Chapter 7

Ruth's truth 33: Seize opportunities to communicate that occur every day.

Ruth's truth 34: Develop an introductory pitch that concisely tells what you do and what's in it for the listener.

Ruth's truth 35: Practice delivering your introductory pitch.

Ruth's truth 36: Determine your main message.

Ruth's truth 37: Define your objective.

Ruth's truth 38: Organize your thoughts by using SALES.

Ruth's truth 39: Use stories to give life to data and information.

Ruth's truth 40: Personal stories are best.

Ruth's truth 41: Transitions and segues facilitate communication by connecting different sections, forming a cohesive unit.

Ruth's truth 42: Notes, used effectively, help to keep you focused and on track, adding to the impression of poise and confidence.

The Big News About Small Talk

Jonathan was complaining to me about how he hated going to his company's social events. He felt that nothing substantive was ever discussed, work was pressing, and his time seemed wasted on discussions that centered on sports, leisure activities, or personal matters. Jonathan was like many people who do not understand the enormous value of small talk. This may have something to do with the label. But small talk is anything but. This type of conversation is a rite that we all must pass through to get to the other, "big talk."

Small talk provides a number of benefits:

- It allows people to feel each other out, with little risk.
- It provides opportunities to find common ground.
- It establishes comfort zones.
- It facilitates the move into "big talk."

Dr. Deborah Tannen, who writes and speaks extensively about small talk, says

> Many moments are spent in casual chat that establishes the friendly working environment that is the necessary backdrop to getting work done. It is easier to approach someone with a work-related issue if you are comfortable in each other's presence and the lines of communication are open. A major way such working relationships are established is through informal, nonwork talk.[1]

People are put off by those who claim to "have no time" for small talk. It conveys a level of self-importance that is discouraging and demoralizing.

This makes good sense because of the topics small talk often centers on

- Family
- Health
- Work
- Hobbies
- Vacations
- Sports
- Politics
- Religion
- Other people (also known as *gossip*)

When we acknowledge how much we learn through small talk, we can begin to imagine how cold and impersonal a workplace or social life would be if there weren't any.

NOTICING WHO'S AROUND YOU

Claire, a group head in a company whose business was dominated by men, was a fabulous speaker and highly regarded by the chief executive and other top managers. Watching her relate to her colleagues was a treat. Claire could walk into a room where she was often the only woman and confidently take her place at the table. When she spoke, there were few interruptions as her coworkers listened intently. And when she gave a presentation, they were as glued and transfixed by her delivery as outsiders were, even though many of them had been deeply involved in the preparation process with her.

I loved working with Claire to fine-tune her presentations because she was always so eager for input, even though she was already quite good. I asked Claire how she came to have such good relationships with all these men. She replied that it had taken a long time and a lot of work to persuade them to accept her. When she first came to the company, she felt isolated and had a difficult time getting anyone to engage in small talk. She then began to listen to the types of things they were talking about. She discovered that one of her close coworkers had a special interest in a musical group. She admitted to me that although she had no interest in that type of music, she felt that she needed to do something to grease the wheels of conversation. So Claire began to read up. She found interesting articles that she clipped and dropped on the coworker's desk. She subscribed the group's Web site e-mail service that sent her updates on the latest releases and concert schedules. She bought a couple of CDs and listened to the music. To her surprise, she even found herself humming some of the tunes. She located a rare recording of one of the musician's work and gave it to her colleague as a gesture of good will. It turned out he already had it, but he was so blown away by the gesture and by the fact that he now had another person he could regale with stories about the musician and the music that they soon became much closer. For Claire it was the first step in a systematic process to curry favor with and get to know the people with whom she spent most days. Once this person accepted her, others took notice and became more accepting as well.

If this sounds like it was a lot of work, it was. Claire spent many hours homing in on her coworkers' interests in an effort to persuade them that she could be one of them, that she wasn't so different. She decided to concentrate first on a coworker who was highly regarded by both peers and superiors. She felt that if she could build a relationship with him, he would make efforts to include her in conversations and social outings with the others in the group. Claire understood the importance of being able to make small talk and how it functions as a type of "motor oil" for the engine that produces the "big talk" of actual work. She noticed her interpersonal surroundings and realized that she had the power to make them favorable.

When we approach situations that require contact and interaction with people, small talk should be a given. As with everything else I talk about in this book, making good small talk requires planning.

CONVERSATIONAL RITUALS

When we walk into a room full of people, two potential scenarios exist:

1. We meet up with someone we know and say something like, "Hi, how are you?"
2. We meet or are introduced to someone we don't know and say, "Hi, it's nice to meet you."

Now think about these same scenarios but this time imagine that you stop after saying, "Hi." You say nothing further. Wouldn't it feel strange? The second parts of these greetings turn them into what are known as *conversational rituals*. When we say, "How are you?" we're not really looking for a long dissertation about the state of that person's health. When we say, "It's nice to meet you," we're not truly thinking that (although it may be true); it's done reflexively, automatically, *without thinking*. Greetings such as these are meant to be polite ways of entering and beginning a conversation that sociolinguists call *conversation smoothers*. They contend that these smoothers make it possible to move the conversation forward. In addition to the ones just mentioned, there are many other greetings that get a lot of use:

"How's it goin'?"
"What's goin' on?"
"What's the word?"
"How ya' doin'?"
"What's up?"(or "Whazzup?" in contemporary parlance)
"Good to meet you!"
"A pleasure to meet you."
"The pleasure is mine."
"Howdy!"

There are loads more, and they vary from region to region. We do not take them literally. They have evolved to be the things that we say in a particular situation. We are evaluated based on how we use them. Imagine a person from another country who hears this talk for the first time. That person would not automatically know that it is a conversational ritual, not meant for literal translation. All countries and cultures have their own conversational rituals that others, outside the native group, may find surprising and be unprepared to deal with.

The next time you greet someone or meet someone new, notice everyone's use of conversational rituals. You will be surprised at the sway these small, not consciously considered verbal exchanges influence the existence and direction of small talk.

READ THE NEWSPAPER

So where do you go after the initial greeting? How many times have you been introduced to someone new or inserted yourself into a conversation and found everyone awkwardly searching for something to say? I regret that this happens to me more often than I would like. So I try to prepare for small talk by reading and have found the best resource to be a large-circulation daily newspaper.

I am addicted to the newspaper. I read it every day no matter where I am or what I am doing. I am so hooked that once, when I was doing a project in Germany, I paid $18 for a Sunday edition of the *New York Times—on Monday!*

There are many things we should all be reading, of course, but if you have time to read only one, the newspaper is the most valuable source of small-talk subjects. Unfortunately, most people get their news from television and radio, which do not provide nearly the in-depth reporting of a newspaper. These media are very limited by time constraints, whereas newspapers can print more pages if there is more news. Taking advantage of this great and readily available resource automatically gives you an edge in making small talk.

Topics vary widely and certainly include all those listed above. Technology has allowed newspapers, especially the big ones, to become very sophisticated. The information superhighway has been a tremendous boon to reporting and newsgathering, allowing instant reporting and analysis on events and people. Newspapers also have made valiant attempts to attract new readers by creating sections that cater to various interests. While there have always been articles on "soft" topics such as cooking and home decorating, newspapers have increased these subjects' stature markedly by devoting entire sections to them each week, profiling stars in the fields and providing information to readers on how to acquire products and skills.

Newspapers are also very readable for most people. Therefore, they are an excellent source of new vocabulary words. Newspapers also use the language of the subjects they are discussing without resorting to jargon, so they are great places to learn how to speak to people in a particular field even if you are not in that field yourself and may not know much about it. Newspapers give you a jumping off point for asking questions that, as you'll find in Chapter 10, are excellent ways to start new or deepen existing conversations.

The part of the newspaper that I read first is the op-ed section. I'm especially interested in the opinion page. In large papers such as the *New York Times,* the *Wall Street Journal,* the *Washington Post,* and the *Los Angeles Times,* great journalists, thinkers, writers, and researchers who comment on current events populate the opinion pages. This is different from reporting, which is not supposed to convey an opinion. Every day these newspapers feature regular opinion columns by journalists who have much insight as a result of the many high-level contacts they have made during the course of their time in the field or covering specialized beats. The best papers give space to both conservative and liberal opinions and many in between. I love to read about diverse points of view.

Editorials tend to reflect the opinions of the newspapers' owners and publishers, which usually lean right or left politically. They are (or should be) balanced by some of the opinions. There is also the occasional humorist or short essay from an unexpected source. The op-ed pages also contain letters to the editor. These letters contain brief comments and opinions on the many topics covered in a given paper and are a great way to find out what readers are thinking. The bottom line is that the op-ed pages provide great fodder for small talk.

Another area to explore in the newspaper is the cartoon section, both regular and political. Cartoons are fantastic ways to communicate. The best political cartoonists are able to fuse a complex concept, opinion, or news story into one picture and caption. The regular comics section often portrays current events tilted more toward social issues. A cartoon I clipped years ago shows a prisoner about to be guillotined being asked by his executioner, "Any last words?" to which the condemned man is shown thinking, "Damn, I hate public speaking." When I show or describe this cartoon to people, it always gets a laugh, identifies me immediately as someone with a sense of humor, and lets them know that they're far from alone in their own feelings about public speaking. All this from one picture! As the old Chinese proverb says, "A picture is worth more than 1000 words."

Although the newspaper I read is widely read and highly regarded, what I would call a "world newspaper," I also read the local paper and advise people to do the same. Local papers are the best sources of what's going on in town and a terrific resource for finding out who's who, who's doing what, who's gotten promoted, who's moved to a new job, who's started a new business, who's contributed an article, who's written a book, and so on. These are the only sources of information regarding local government or schools, issues that are crucial for residents to know about. And of course, there are the specialty newspapers designed to convey information about a particular field. Everyone should be a subscriber to their own industry publications because they are the best sources of relevant business news. Finally, there are the big weekly national newsmagazines, including *Time, Newsweek, BusinessWeek,* and a couple of others that cover current events weekly. These are also good sources of information, although they are not as extensive or as current as newspapers.

By the way, I like to have the hard copy to read, but if you prefer to access a newspaper or magazine online or happen to live in an area where a hard copy isn't readily available, you can subscribe to most of these publications on the Internet.

Then there are the clippings that newspapers are the best source of. In addition to keeping a file of your own, clippings can be forwarded to clients and associates. Doing this practically begs for responses and thus provides opportunities for small (or big) talk. Statistics, company information, the latest science and medical news, and recipes—newspapers have it all. Today, with periodicals available online, articles can be "clipped" electronically and e-mailed to specific parties. I maintain a vast file of newspaper and magazine clippings going back nearly 20 years. I am always adding to the file. When necessary, I go through the file to find material to support a presentation or written piece. Because I've been doing it for so long, I now possess a historical perspective on many issues. My friend Donna Daniels, the well-known film publicist, noting how I comment or have information on so many topics, often has teased me over the years by saying, "Ruthie, you know everything!" While this is hardly true, I do know a little about a great many things, and it's all because I read the paper.

Reading up on current events, getting other perspectives by reading opinions and editorials, and enjoying cartoons will help to make you a more worldly and interesting conversationalist. This will give you the power to easily engage in the small talk that forms the basic structure necessary to carry a conversation forward.

Ruth's Rules for Chapter 8

Ruth's truth 43: Small talk facilitates the move into "big talk."

Ruth's truth 44: Conversational rituals are the basis for small talk.

Ruth's truth 45: Read as much as possible, but especially large newspapers.

Ruth's truth 46: Clip articles and keep them in a file to which you can refer.

Listen Well and They'll Eat Out of Your Hand

As I am writing this chapter, my 10-year-old daughter and her best friend are playing boisterously nearby. I try to get a word in to no avail. So I resort to shouting, "Listen!" Old habits die hard.

Everything I've spoken about so far has to do with sending information. But there is another side to the communication equation: receiving information, or listening. In Chapter 1, I talked about people like Oprah Winfrey and Barbara Walters who have the ability to make others feel special and open up. Watching them do their work, it becomes apparent that not only are they good at sending their messages, but they are also good at receiving messages from others. As Susan RoAne says in her book, *What Do I Say Next? Talking Your Way to Business and Social Success*, "No one goes around saying 'I really like my doctor. . . . You ought to use him. He doesn't listen to me!'"[1]

It is well-known fact among communication professionals and scholars that listening is the most important *and the most neglected* communication skill. Of the four skills that we use to communicate—talking, writing, reading, and listening—listening takes the prize for getting the most use. Unfortunately, although it may be used widely, it is also used poorly.

Becoming a good listener, however, is a terrific way to gain attention and get people to see things your way precisely because it is so rare to find someone who listens well. Human beings find great comfort in being listened to. When we find a good listener, we take notice. We advertise this fact when referring to that person or recommending that person to some-one else. We look for opportunities to be around that person.

It's understandable, really. Training in communication skills is scarce, and when we do receive it, it usually focuses on speaking—how to be heard, how to present, how to give a speech, how to interrupt—the programs and book titles are numerous. I believe that this is somewhat the result of our show business–obsessed culture, the value we place on good presentation skills, on being out there performing. Speaking is obvious, loud, in your face. Listening, on the other hand, is subtle and quiet—very quiet.

PLUGGING IN BY LISTENING

A movie I recently saw had a funny scene. One character was speaking, and the other was listening, making eye contact, every so often muttering "Yeah" or "Uh-huh," leaning in and tilting his head, and furrowing his brow. After a minute or so, the speaker, in frustration, blurted out, "Stop your active listening! I hate active listening!" to which the listener replied, "I can listen and be an active listener at the same time."

The idea of active listening certainly has been in the forefront of workforce education and research in recent years. The philosophy behind the active listening movement is that it is hard work and must be engaged in energetically, like speaking. There are behaviors active listeners should exhibit, such as making listening noises ("Yes," "Uh-huh," "I see," etc.), lis-tening movements (cocking the head, furrowing the brow, nodding, etc.), and not allowing interruptions or judgmental thoughts to intrude. Unfortunately, due to the ubiquity of listening workshops and graduates of them practicing these same techniques, active listening is at risk of becom-ing a parody of itself. At worst, it smacks of insincerity and of exhibiting "listening behaviors" instead of actually listening. The thing is that they both take time and energy, so why not try the latter and reap the benefits that real listening provides?

I do not buy into the notion that listening is hard work. I love listening and find it to be relaxing and enjoyable. It is good break from speaking. I also find it to be tremendously rewarding because I *learn so much*. Listening to people is a marvelous way to find out things about them, about others, about the business, and about the social universe.

On the other hand, listening is not a passive act. We live in a noisy, distracting world with which we are always competing. Yet the art of listening should be part of the ebb and flow of communication. I go back to the idea that you've got to like people and be interested in them and in what they have to say for true listening to take place.

During a recent presidential election campaign, I was at a political fundraiser in Washington at which a number of political luminaries were present. One person, a candidate for high national office, worked the room, shaking hands, making eye contact, and standing dutifully for "photo ops." He was trying hard, but there was something missing. Perhaps it was the assembly-line quality to it. He couldn't seem to connect or give his full attention to anyone for the minute or two they were engaged in conversation.

Another individual, a well-known and senior party leader and strategist, after being introduced to people, literally turned his back on some of them as if to say that they were not worthy of his time. That year, a major election year, the party was soundly defeated. Although probably not the only reason, the unwillingness to master listening (among other important communication skills) just didn't seem to be a high priority with this group and certainly contributed to their rout.

I do not argue that any of these busy, important people should have spent undue amounts of time listening to any single individual at this event. People who attend these events know the drill; they are mindful of candidates' limited time and grateful for any amount of time they can spare. But even in just a few seconds or minutes, a great amount of listening can be accomplished and a binding connection made.

LISTEN TO UNDERSTAND

The most basic of all human needs is the need to understand and be understood. The best way to understand people is to listen to them.
—Ralph Nichols

Listening to understand is a good place to start becoming a skillful listener. When we listen with an underlying desire to understand, we focus on what is being said and attempt to come up with appropriate responses. When we listen to understand, we automatically make eye contact, listening noises, facial expressions, and gestures that indicate that we are engaged and present. When we are not engaged as listeners, we don't achieve the understanding. Often we don't even remember what is said.

I always know when I'm not listening. It often rears its ugly head when I'm introduced to someone new and I don't remember the person's name immediately after hearing it. (This is almost always because I'm more concerned with the impression *I'm* making than with the other individual.) I know a good many people have trouble remembering the names of people they've just been introduced to, but few of them attribute that to poor listening—perhaps because it is so widespread. But poor listening is exactly what it is, and there isn't a better illustration.

There is no such thing as a perfect listener, much the same as there is no such thing as a perfect speaker. These are human skills and, as a result, are very flawed in their execution. I don't think that it's productive to give out a prescription for how to be a good, active listener (others are already on that bandwagon). I do think that it's helpful to provide a list of things to beware of, warnings that all may not be going well in the listening arena at any given moment.

Warning Signs of Personal Listening Loss

- Forgetting someone's name immediately after being introduced
- Thinking of something unrelated while you should be listening
- Interrupting too often
- Imagining what that person would be like in . . . (Yes, it does happen and means you're not listening.)
- Asking a speaker to repeat himself or herself
- Yawning and exhibiting other signs of boredom

Warning Signs of Others' Listening Loss

- Looking around the room as if for a better opportunity
- Forgetting your name immediately after being introduced
- Turning the conversation back to himself or herself
- Not giving appropriate responses
- No nonverbal indications that listening is taking place

- Interrupting too often
- Not reacting or reacting inappropriately, such as laughing at the wrong moment
- Yawning and exhibiting other signs of boredom

THE LISTENING LEVELS

Being able to listen well requires becoming aware of the different ways in which we listen. We're not always listening intently, nor do we always have to be. For example, when I'm in the car with the radio on, I'm listening to news or music. Since I don't have to respond to the radio (although I know people who do), I naturally do not listen with that in mind. I also find that I have to turn the radio off when I'm trying to focus on a particularly difficult driving situation, such as finding my way somewhere. At those moments, I can't listen. When I listen to friends and family members, the way I listen depends on what they are saying. If they are talking about their day or other casual, routine conversation, I listen in one way. If one of them comes to me and says that she needs to talk about something, well that's another type of listening entirely. (I have to be very careful here; sometimes something will be said under the guise of casual speech that is important and requires more than casual listening.) Another situation is listening while doing business. In this case I am always trying to listen intently because my time with clients is so precious. I know that if I don't listen, I may miss something very important. We all adapt our listening behaviors to the given situation. Knowing about the different types of listening can help you to choose one that will work for a particular situation. Listening has been classified into three levels primarily due to the work of Madelyn Burley-Allen.[2] My version of the listening levels follows starting with level 3:

Level 3: Hearing but Not Listening

The situation I just described with me in my car listening to the radio is a stark example of level 3 listening. I'm *hearing* words and music, but I'm not *listening*. This type of listening does not require thinking or responding. I can tune in and out as I see fit. I don't have to try to be understanding or sympathetic to the speaker. Another situation that could be described as level 3 is a situation I fell into with my former friend Allison, who could talk and talk without taking a breather (see "Dealing with an Audience of One" later on in this chapter.). A final example of level 3 listening comes at those moments when you are deeply involved in a task or are watching television and someone walks into the room and begins speaking to you. One reaction is to say "Uh-huh" or make other listening noises that indicate that you may be listening. Another is no reaction at all because the truth is that you're not listening.

Level 2: Casual Listening

When we move our efforts up a notch, we are devoting more of our cognitive powers to the act of listening—of taking in information and formulating responses. The missing link in casual listening is the emotional connection. We are not in it to learn something, or we are just having fun. We are able tune in and out without risk. If something catches our ear, we may ask for it to be repeated. Perhaps the person speaking is boring or taking up too much of our time. Maybe we've got something else on our mind that is taking up the space we need to listen more intently. We even fake it sometimes, leaving people believing that we are listening when we are not.

Level 1: Intent Listening

A fundamental interpersonal skill in the moral development of human beings is empathy. *Empathy* is the ability to identify with and understand another's situation, feelings, and motives. It's when you put yourself in the shoes of the other person. Empathy is a great route to imagining what another person is going through and a great aid to meeting their needs. Empathy is also a crucial component of intent or level 1 listening. Empathetic or intent listening is the listening we should use when we are required to respond. Burley-Allen believes that it should be the listening we are always striving for in every situation. I don't agree. I think that it is too much work and unnecessary to be an intent, empathetic listener all the time. It risks turning people off to the act entirely. However, there are certain situations where intent listening is mandatory. These include the times when friends or family ask you to listen to them and in just about every business situation.

Intent listening delivers the following benefits:

- It builds self-esteem in the person who is being listened to.
- It heightens others' regard of the listener.
- It encourages creative thinking.
- It bolsters one's ability to gather information.
- It builds and nourishes relationships.
- It leads to questioning and clarifying.

There are also some basic rules:

- Give your full attention.
- Resist the urge to interrupt, except to ask for clarification.
- Leave your value judgments at the door.
- Do not allow external interruptions.
- If your mind begins to wander, exercise discipline and bring it back. Ask the person to repeat anything you may have missed.

Becoming an intent level 1 listener takes practice (so what else is new?). Practice your skills with your close friends or family, and then bring those skills to your business. If you keep in mind both the benefits and the rules listed above, your experience should bear some very ripe fruit.

WHEN LISTENING IS A LOSER: DEALING WITH SPECIAL SITUATIONS

There are occasions when we waste time listening. Conversation is a two-way street, so there is a responsibility by all parties to strike a balance between listening and speaking. It is not the sole responsibility of any one party to hold up both ends of a conversation. Listening is only half the equation. The speaker must tune into the listener's capacity for taking it in. Too many speakers do not read the reactions of people whom they expect to listen to them, and they are at high risk of being left in the dust at business and social gatherings. No one wants to stand and listen to someone who is oblivious to the needs of others. It's a challenge to find a way to extricate yourself. If you are feeling monopolized, however, it pays to have some escape routes.

There *are* times when we have to stick around even when the speaker is boring. When this happens, most often with clients, bosses, and some colleagues, it pays to reframe your thought process. Instead of thinking, "This is so boring; I can't wait to get out of here," which blocks all the messages being conveyed, think, "I need this person to do my job, so what can I learn that will help me?" By rethinking the process, you dispense with a good deal of negative energy and can extract important information you didn't have before.

Dealing with an Audience of One

During my first career as a performer in New York, I had a friend who loved to talk, and talk, and talk. Allison was always looking for advice for her career, love life, family life—you name it. And I was one of those people who loved to give advice but never asked for any. We were a perfect pair. One evening, during one of our many phone "conversations" when Allison was talking and I was listening, I decided to conduct an experiment. I set down the phone and did a few dishes in the sink. When I returned a few minutes later, Allison was still talking. She never knew I had been gone. I knew at that moment that our friendship had taken a decidedly negative turn and that things would have to change. I decided that if she didn't even need verbal acknowledgment that I was there, still listening, making those listening noises, she really didn't need me at all. What I realized she liked most was the sound of her own voice and a captive audience.

Listening to a Fault: Not Holding Up Your End of a Conversation

On the other side of the coin are those who seem to do nothing *but* listen. These people seem to float above it all, never reacting verbally, offering advice, or asking questions. They fancy themselves good listeners or else quiet and reserved. Often they are truly shy and feel awkward in conversation. Whatever the reason, though, the result is that they are not holding up their end of the conversation.

When approached about why they have so little to add, the answer they often give is that unless they have something important to contribute, they prefer to stay out of a conversation. Unfortunately, this methodology can backfire; others will misinterpret their actions, ascribing their behavior to aloofness, disengagement, or worse—incompetence or inability. Listening is successful only if people know that you are doing it—if they can *feel* it.

If shyness has gotten the better of you, make some plans to speak up—just to be heard. There are worse reasons.

By using good listening skills, you will communicate that you care about and respect what your client or customer is saying. The more you show that you care, the better your relationship will become, the more open a client or customer will be, and the more likely it is that you will be able to overcome objections and get that person to see things your way.

Listening well, knowing how to apply the various types of listening, and understanding that intent listening is not a passive act can be a great boon to business and social success. Good listeners are hard to find—we know it when we find one. Become a good listener, and you'll be amazed at the relationships you'll be able to build—and quickly. In a crowded, noisy world, being a good listener is definitely a way to stand out. After all, people gotta' eat—it might as well be out of your hand.

Ruth's Truths for Chapter 9

Ruth's truth 47: Listening is critical to success and very rarely done well.

Ruth's truth 48: Good listeners are hard to find.

Ruth's truth 49: Listening is relaxing, fun, and very interesting.

Ruth's truth 50: Strive for level 1, intent listening in important personal relationships and in business.

What Questions Do You Have?

Judge a man by his questions, rather than his answers.

—Voltaire

I read recently about an employer who interviews applicants in an unusual way. He gives a one-minute presentation about the company and then asks the prospective employee, "What questions do you have?" He believes that the ability to ask good questions is indicative of an active and creative mind. He also believes that if you can ask good questions, you can find good answers, interpreting that to mean that a candidate would be a good problem solver, an asset in any business.

ASKING GOOD QUESTIONS

So what makes a good question? I think of good, high-quality questions as seeds that can be planted to make a conversation grow. When the conversation grows, information results, and the more information we have, the better able we are to make good decisions. It doesn't matter what the topic is. Good, high-quality questions always will result in the best information coming forth.

People often are timid about asking the right questions. They seem to be reluctant to dig too deeply or to probe in an area they think of as off limits. By thinking this way, we often limit ourselves instead. People love to talk, and they interpret questioning, if it is done correctly, as evidence of interest on the part of the person doing the asking. The person asking the questions controls the conversation, and the better the questions, the better the control.

For certain professions, the ability to question is critical and displays the mastery the professional may have. The professions that come to mind most prominently are that of psychotherapist, medical doctor or other health-care provider, and law-enforcement professional. Think of a forensic physician or arson investigator. It is impossible to imagine these people being able to do their jobs without being able to ask clear, direct, and perhaps unorthodox or unexpected questions.

OPEN VERSUS CLOSED QUESTIONING

Every day my children can be sure of one thing: I'm going to ask them how their day was. The exchange usually goes something like this:

Mom: "So, how was your day today?"
Child: "Good."
Mom: "What did you do?"
Child: "Nothing."

There's not much information there. Like a lot of parents, I get a bit frustrated when I talk to my kids. I want to know how things are going, but I don't want to come across desperate (which I am). They are tired, having been in school all day, and don't feel much like reviewing the day with me. Besides, they probably want to have a little fun pushing my buttons. My desperation combined with their fatigue and button-pushing tendencies do not add up to good information. This leaves me feeling disconnected from my children. I can remember the same thing happening with my parents, and I don't want to repeat it.

A few years ago I decided to try to apply some of the communication techniques that I spend a good deal of time thinking about each and every day. (It's funny how when we're close to people, all that good training and experience go flying out the window.) My first thought was that my timing was off. I certainly did not want to launch into a description of my own day on arriving home, so why did I expect my children to? I decided to find a better time, such as just before bedtime when we were both feeling more relaxed and lovey-dovey. Then I thought that perhaps I should rephrase my questions so that they weren't the same ones I had been asking day after day:

Mom: "So, what did you learn about today?"
Child: "Nothing much."

Finally, I got more than a one-word answer, so I began to probe:

Mom: "What are you working on in science?"
Child: "We're learning about the solar system."
Mom: "What is the solar system?"
Child: "It's when there's a star, like our Sun, that planets like Earth revolve around."
Mom: "I'd like to know what you're learning about in social studies."
Child: "We're learning about the equator and prime meridian and those lines and circles on the earth."
Mom: "Oh, latitude and longitude and the Arctic and Antarctic circles?
Child: "Yup."

And so on. The exchange is productive. It elicits information and allows for follow-up questions. I also have realized that I don't have to ask questions every day. Not every school day is action-packed. Two or three times a week is sufficient, with one of those times being on the weekend.

The difference between the first question I asked:

"So, how was your day today?"

and a more specific question:

"What are you learning about in science?"

is that the first one is closed and the second one is open. *Closed questions* require only a one-word or very brief answer.[1] *Open questions* are designed to elicit information. There is a place for both, but in most cases, if you're looking for high-quality information, if you want to control the direction of the conversation, you should attempt to ask open questions.

Examples of open questions include

"How did you accomplish that task?"
"Tell me about yourself."
"Where do things stand with the project?"
"What do you expect the department to look like after the training?"
"Tell me about the culture of the organization."
"Why do you want to leave your current position?"
"Where do you see yourself in five years?"
"How will you know you've succeeded?"
"What's your assessment of the situation?"
"How did you fare during the merger?"
"What do you think about joining our department?"

All these questions encourage the responder to open up, to provide information that the questioner can then use to decide what question to ask next. People interviewing candidates for jobs, as well as the professionals mentioned in the preceding section, use the open style of questioning almost exclusively.

Closed questions do not encourage the release of a lot of information. Often the answers are either yes or no. But they have their place, especially in the conversational rituals we all use to grease the wheels of conversation:

"How are you?"
"What's the weather like?"
"Is it cold out today?"
"Have you ever been here before?"
"Are you going to the party?"
"Would you like to get some lunch?"
"When will you be returning?"
"How was school today?"
"Are you hungry?"

These types of questions facilitate definite answers and provide clarity as to a person's feelings. For those reasons they are useful.

CLARIFYING: CHECKING FOR UNDERSTANDING

Clarifying questions are used when an answer is not as coherent as you might hope. When you are listening to understand (see Chapter 9*)*, moments will occur when you must ask questions that will facilitate that understanding:

> "Let me make sure that I hear you correctly. What you're saying is. . . ?"
> "So, if I am to understand, you agree that . . . ?"
> "I'm not sure I understand. You said that...?"
> "It's important that I get this right. Are you saying that . . .?"
> "If we could step back for a moment, would you please explain that again?"

Teachers are among the biggest recipients of clarifying questions.

SEEKING AGREEMENT FOR NEXT STEPS

When we seek agreement to take further steps, we are gaining partners in a process. The more people we can persuade to join us in a given venture, the more likely we will be to succeed. Some people call this *preselling.* I think that's a little bit like George Carlin's humorous take on the phrase "preboarding" that the airlines use. Perhaps *advance selling* or *influencing* is a more accurate term. However you may choose to view it, the more attempts we make to get people on board with our ideas and strategies, the more likely we are to get people over to our way of thinking and to take those crucial next steps to achieving our aims.

Catherine, an executive in a large insurance and financial services company, wanted some coaching. It seemed that she had a great many good ideas but couldn't seem to sell any of them to either her bosses or her colleagues. She felt that her presentation skills were good, that she was well organized, and that her ideas were timely and creative. Her strategy had been to wait until she had a meeting to bring up an idea. Then one of three things typically would happen:

- The idea would be discussed briefly and then tossed out.
- The idea would be discussed more fully but be torn apart and then tossed out.

- The idea would be ignored. Then it would be revisited a few weeks or months later, but credit would be given to someone else.

I asked her if she ever ran ideas by her bosses and/or coworkers before the meetings. She said no. She was reluctant to share her ideas beforehand because she was afraid they'd either be stolen or shot down before she got a chance to present them to the larger group. I concurred that there were risks, but I suggested that there were benefits, too. I told her that sharing her ideas with coworkers whom she trusted before going into meetings could have very positive effects:

- She would get feedback that could improve the ideas.
- She would gain allies, which she needed.
- She would have a good chance of getting her ideas taken seriously, leading to the next steps.

The only downside was that credit would have to be shared somewhat. She agreed to give it a shot. She began to run her ideas by certain trusted colleagues. This took place informally, with Catherine casually stopping by someone's office or grabbing a coworker's attention in one of the public spaces at the company or during informal meals and breaks.

One thing that was of great concern to Catherine was the very real risk that her ideas would be coopted by a colleague. Much as she trusted and liked these people and had no problem sharing some of the credit, she knew that the more she shared and the longer the time lag before the meeting, the more title to her ideas would become blurred. She wanted management to know that the original idea was hers. To ensure that things would remain in her control, we put in place a communication strategy whereby Catherine obtained agreement from her coworkers that she would be the lead presenter of the idea. She would introduce it, beginning with words like

> I have an idea for [describe idea] that I'd like to get your input on. Mike, Carol, Jessica, and I have been tossing it around the past few weeks, and we have come up with some strategies for implementation.

Then each of the colleagues would take a turn presenting their portion of the concept that improved on Catherine's original idea.

By employing a strategy to gain agreement and allies before springing the idea at the meeting, Catherine was in a much better position to get her idea heard and the next steps implemented. Not only did she get the primary credit for the idea, but Catherine also became someone to whom her colleagues came when *they* needed some backup. By including her friends and colleagues, she built closer bonds with them.

The idea of seeking agreement so that the next steps can be taken is, once again, a strategy that takes some preparation and planning. The efforts can be intense, but so are the rewards.

Questioning, probing, asking for support, and seeking agreement are marvelous methods of building lasting relationships. They are the only ways I know of to get people talking and to uncover information that may be deeply buried. Skilled questioners get better answers. Better answers confer a competitive advantage.

ANY OBJECTIONS?

When was the last time you heard an objection from a client or customer? Better yet, when was the last time you raised an objection yourself? If you're like most people, the answer will be "very recently." The most frequent objections these days result from calls by telemarketers. I know that I rarely buy from these people, and my objections usually state just that: "I don't buy over the phone."

It is critical to know that dealing with objections is part of the process of winning people over. Just like the sales presentation and other facets of the operation, objections can be planned for and overcome. Fortunately, objections are limited, and because of this, you can prepare to deal with them.

Objections trip up a lot of people for three reasons:

1. People take them personally.
2. People don't plan for them.
3. People don't practice handling them.

Let's look at the reasons that objections often derail the selling process one by one. The first, *taking objections personally*, is one that may feel familiar to you. Objections feel like personal rejections to some people (see Chapter 16). When a customer or client says, "I'm not interested," especially if they say it in a rude or abrupt way, it can feel as if that customer has decided that it is you, not your product or service, that is being sidelined. However, if you've done your homework, qualified your prospect, and worked on your presentation, the objection may be many things, but it is *not* personal. When an objection feels personal, the immediate gut reaction is to withdraw. This reaction will put a halt to the selling process and make it difficult to impossible to return to that client or customer. However, if you view an objection as an opportunity to learn more about a client and his or her needs, then real progress can be made.

The second reason, *lack of planning,* is as unfortunate as it is unnecessary. And it's an old, persistent part of the communication environment. Dealing successfully with objections takes planning. This is a place where colleagues and friends can help. Being able to anticipate the types of objections that are likely to be raised encourages you to have answers ready. No one can anticipate every objection that may arise, but you can anticipate and prepare for the vast majority of them. In my work, I have found that people who anticipate and plan for dealing with objections accurately predict over 90 percent of them. Following are the objections that are received most often:

"The price is too high."
"We don't have the budget."
"Send us your literature."
"We already have a relationship with another supplier."
"We don't have a need for these services/products."

There are others, but these are the most common.

The third reason, *lack of practice*, is directly related to the preceding two. If you take objections personally and back off, you will never give yourself the chance to practice overcoming them. If you do not plan and prepare for objections, there will be no opportunities to practice responding to them.

Objections are wonderful occasions to practice questioning skills discussed earlier in this chapter. When a client raises an objection, that person is actually creating an opening for you to probe and find out more about the client and his or her actual needs. One of the most common objections has to do with the price being too high. When this happens, most salespeople don't know what to say, so they begin ticking off all the reasons why the price is fair. Instead, the salesperson should do a little probing: "Can you tell me why you think the price is too high?" At that point you are beginning a process that may get you to the real reason the objection was raised. Perhaps the client's budget won't accommodate such a price. Or maybe the client doesn't understand how the price relates to the service or product being discussed. If you don't ask, you won't know. Once the real reason is uncovered, you had better be prepared to explain your pricing strategy and the value that it brings. Price objections always should be number one on the list of anticipated barriers. It is natural, after all, for clients and customers to explore ways to hold down costs. Remember to ask probing, open questions, not closed ones, so that you can get the client talking.

Once the client begins talking, you must begin listening. Intent level 1 listening is the order of the day (see Chapter 9).

Ruth's Truths for Chapter 10

Ruth's truth 51: Questions are the seeds of conversation.

Ruth's truth 52: Open questions elicit more information than closed questions.

Ruth's truth 53: Questions control the conversation.

Ruth's truth 54: Seek agreement through advance selling.

Ruth's truth 55: Objections are opportunities to ask questions and uncover hidden needs.

Ruth's truth 56: Anticipate objections and prepare answers.

Once More with Feeling: Making the Emotional Connection

The ability to display emotion when communicating is one of the most important skills a communicator must have. Putting feelings into what you're saying by using nonverbal communication as a conduit for your emotions and to stir the emotions of others is key to connecting with your audience. As a listener, too, there is a responsibility to show that you are taking in the information being offered to you and that you care about what is being said.

Too many of us have been trained to withhold or hide our emotions. In certain circles, showing emotions is considered bad form. Emotional manifestations often are considered to be unprofessional. I'm not recommending that you burst into tears or display other behaviors that may be considered to be extreme and embarrassing. However, to communicate successfully, you must be willing to take some risks.

WITHHOLD EMOTIONS AT YOUR OWN RISK

A notorious example of the harm that can result from a reluctance to show emotions occurred when Michael Dukakis, the former governor of Massachusetts, was running for president. An opponent of the death penalty, he was asked during a nationally televised debate if he would still feel the same way if his wife were raped and murdered. His response was widely perceived to be so technical, "policy-centric," and lacking in emotion that viewers became turned off to him. The media had a field day.

Although he had been well ahead in the polls, his numbers began to slip, and he never recovered. George Bush, Sr., won the election, a man not known, by any means, as having a great emotional range. Dukakis lost sight of the importance of connecting emotionally with voters. Since the defeat of George Bush, Sr., by Bill Clinton and the ensuing presidency of the second George Bush, how well a candidate connects with the electorate has been instrumental in winning elections. And it just happened again in California, where the incumbent Gray Davis, who seemed to inspire widespread disaffection by almost everyone who came into contact with him, was replaced by Arnold Schwarzenegger, a movie star with lots of charisma and no political experience.

SCARED STRAIGHT

We've all known people who, reluctant to show how they feel, speak in a monotone voice with a stiff physical presence. Often they read their information. These folks normally have good data, the material is well researched, and it is much needed by their listeners. But they fear becoming intimate with others, of exposing their feelings. They are literally scared straight. And because of this fear of exposure, they subsequently fail to communicate their messages. Some of these fears are the result of early training. Their parents may have told them that public displays of emotion were unseemly or poor manners. Others fear coming off as too slick. Many of my clients have expressed concerns about coming off as too "salesy" or theatrical.

I am reminded of one client, a large, prestigious private bank, that was planning to take some select, very wealthy clients on a retreat to a luxury resort where these clients would attend workshops on financial planning and investing led by these bankers. The bankers were very concerned about the possibility that their clients might perceive them as "selling" too much. My response was that the wealthy people who had accepted the bank's invitation were busy people who did not need a free vacation. The reason they were there was to hear about the services and products the bank had to offer. Protecting financial assets is a major preoccupation of the rich, and they are always looking for new ways keep more of what they earn. They are motivated consumers of financial services. *They want to be sold!* Once the private bankers realized this, they felt much freer to show how passionate they were about their services and products, and the retreat was a big success.

There are three questions you should ask yourself when you are trying to inject some emotion into what you are saying:

- Do you believe and are you committed to what you are speaking about?
- Would you take your own advice?
- Are you willing to get out of your comfort zone?

If you believe what you are speaking about, it shouldn't be too difficult to identify the feelings and commitment that accompany that belief and incorporate those feelings into your vocal and physical display.

The second question asks you to put yourself in your listener's shoes, to use empathy. This is something that as communicators we must all do all the time, and it is an incredibly difficult task. It's tough to be objective. If you are the type of person who practices what you preach, however, you should be able to do an honest assessment.

The third question may be the most important. This is where risk is involved. No one likes to be rejected or disapproved of (see Chapter 16). And if you have been in the habit of concealing your emotions and feelings, it is difficult to change. The real risk, though, is in not being willing or able to demonstrate your commitment by showing others how you feel.

GOOD VERSUS GREAT VIA NONVERBAL COMMUNICATION

I was watching a friend of mine speak at an event. I had seen her before and always enjoyed hearing what she had to say. I was impressed with how well the presentation was thought out, prepared, written. It had all the right elements, and my friend had been growing steadily in reputation as a speaker over the years, something that had become her life's ambition. The next day I called her to thank and congratulate her again. But this time, instead of leaving it at that, I offered to help her begin to take the next steps toward realizing her dream. These were the things that would make her great as opposed to very good. She was eager for my input but admitted that she also had some trepidation. I knew where she was coming from. So I used my trademark, *TLC—Tender Loving Criticism* (see Chapter 4), and gently told her how I thought at this point it was all about spit and polish. And by the way, polishing never ends. I told her that with some polish she could take her presentation to the next level. As is true with most polishing efforts, the feedback I had to offer was centered entirely around nonverbal communication.

Nonverbal Communication Makes Us Believable

The importance of solid nonverbal communication cannot be overstated. Nonverbal communication is what makes us believable. It's what identifies us as genuine and authentic. It gives our words meaning. All the research has shown—and continues to show—that when we speak, we will only be believed if our *nonverbal message is consistent with the verbal one.* I have a great time demonstrating this to participants in my workshops and seminars. While the introduction is being read (which I always provide my hosts and is glowing—and true!), I stand off to the side and look uncomfortable. I don't smile or make eye contact with the audience. I fidget and wring my hands. I then go up to a podium, hang onto it for dear life, and pull out a sheaf of papers half an inch thick containing a good deal of typewritten prose, single spaced, in 12-point font. At this point, as you might imagine, the audience begins to get nervous. I can hear the restless movements. I then begin my presentation, pretending I am reading from my "prepared script." I read words that say I am an expert in communication and that if a communicator is boring, no one will listen to what she says. I purposely keep my voice monotonous. I hem and haw and clear my throat a lot. I make reading errors and redo them.

This all happens over the course of a minute of two. Before anyone gets up to leave, I look up, take the "script," move away from the podium to center stage, drop it into a strategically placed wastebasket, and smile. The sighs of relief are audible. It is a highly effective demonstration of verbal communication (words) not being consistent with nonverbal communication. The audience has the instinctive human reaction of believing what they see and hear in my voice and not what is said. What they see is someone who is clearly no expert speaker. They tune out my words. And they are right to do so.

Show Your Commitment with Good Nonverbal Skills

How we look and sound when communicating telegraphs to others the level of passion and commitment we feel about what we are saying. Nonverbal communication is defined as the communicating we do that does not include the words themselves. These skills are critical differentiators that can make the difference when you attempt to get people to see things your way in a very short time. The nonverbal communication skills that are most important are

- Body movement (posture, stance, stride, hand gestures, etc.)
- Facial expression
- Eye contact
- Voice (tone, inflection, volume, rate, accent/dialect)
- Dress and adornment (everything you weren't born wearing)
- Touch
- Time
- Space

People are often surprised to see touch listed until I mention shaking hands. The same is true for time (appropriate levels of punctuality) and space (proximity to others and relationship of our location to others). How we use these codes communicates a great deal.

The first five nonverbal skills are the ones with which people tend to be most concerned. There is good reason for this: They are the primary methods people have to convey confidence. Our posture needs to be good and our stride purposeful as we walk over to say hello using a strong and expressive voice. We also make eye contact and smile. In other words, we need to look and sound poised and assured. On the phone, of course, voice is paramount because it is the only nonverbal tool we have to use. People extrapolate from the way we look and sound, in effect deciding that if we look and sound good, then we also must *be* good at our work. It is an evolutionary instinct that is connected to finding a suitable mate and, as such, runs very deep. So it is not without reason that we communicate this way.

The astonishing fact is that 93 percent of any spoken message is communicated nonverbally! According to UCLA professor and communication researcher Albert Mehrabian, speech communication can be divided into three parts: the *verbal* (what we say—the words, content), the *vocal* (how we sound), and the *visual* (how we look). How is this possible? Well, just think of things we do every day such as shrugging our shoulders or nodding our heads without ever uttering a single word. We give thumbs up—or down. And these are only a few examples! Perhaps you can't get your arms around the 93 percent figure. Let's say that you believe that the three V's carry equal weight. That still means that 66 percent of the meaning derived from our speech is nonverbal. These numbers ought to get your attention.

Do a Nonverbal Self-Analysis

Nonverbal skills are notoriously difficult to self-assess. Much of what we do nonverbally is unconscious, so we remain blissfully unaware of how we come across. We acquire habits over many years of communicating, and we are given many negative messages about how we should behave interpersonally.

Yet, in order to improve, we must attain a high level of self-awareness. Because of this, it's critical to get feedback. This can be accomplished in a few ways. One method is to use videotape, audiotape, or both. Due to the informal nature of small meetings and informal encounters, though, recording is not as pragmatic as it is for rehearsing a speech or presentation.

Another practical method is to ask for critiques from others. These must be from people who are not afraid to be honest. Coworkers are best because they see you in action. Good, constructive, truthful criticism about nonverbal skills sometimes can be painful, but it is invaluable and the key to improvement. Some people find family members helpful in this area. Others have bosses who are able to give honest, gentle feedback. Still others have employees on whom they can rely. We must each make decisions in this regard, but whomever we choose must be able to give us the pure, unvarnished truth.

Another tremendous benefit of nonverbal communication is that it helps us to *think*. For example, if you observe yourself and others while engaged in informal conversation, people are always gesturing. They aren't thinking about their hands, worrying where they are and what they look like, but their hands help them think. According to Dr. Susan Goldin-Meadow of the University of Chicago, if there is a culture that does not use hands to communicate, it has not been discovered yet. She also notes that even deaf people gesture, in addition to signing.[1]

As with all communication, nonverbal codes must be adjusted to the audience. My husband, Brad Olsen-Ecker, a brilliant graphic artist who has accomplished the feat of having worked steadily in the advertising industry for his entire career, attributes a good deal of his success to his ability to "read the room." By this he means being attuned to and behaving in ways that make people comfortable. Investment bankers require a different nonverbal approach than people in the entertainment industry.

Allowing your feelings to show won't make you seem "salesy" or theatrical but *real*. That authenticity will allow you to connect with your listeners and help you to communicate your messages in a way that will keep them coming back to you for more.

Ruth's Truths for Chapter 11

Ruth's truth 57: You must make an emotional connection to communicate successfully.

Ruth's truth 58: Emotions are communicated nonverbally.

Ruth's truth 59: Nonverbal communication helps you to think.

Ruth's truth 60: To be believable, the verbal and nonverbal messages must be consistent with and not contradict each other.

Ruth's truth 61: Do a nonverbal self-assessment.

Ruth's truth 62: Read the room. Nonverbal communication must be attuned to the audience.

Practice Pointers for Polished Pitches

Jack Mitchell, the retailer and author I quoted in Chapter 5, notes that to be successful and achieve your goals, "You have to plan, practice and prepare," a process he labels the "three P's."[1] I couldn't agree more.

You may recall that in Chapter 3 I mentioned that although Henry Kissinger and Alan Greenspan are not the most wonderful speakers, I suspect that they have preparation down to a science. The issue of practice and rehearsal generally gets short shrift in today's hectic world. This has resulted in a number of problems. People find that they are too busy to take the necessary time to prepare. Unprepared communicators are not able to convey their messages, leaving listeners confused and/or bored. They perhaps fail to understand or grasp that listeners' time is precious, too. When someone takes the time to listen to you, they are hoping to take something away. If they do not, they may be left feeling that their time was wasted, that they didn't get what they came for. To be unprepared is a cardinal sin.

In the years that I've I been coaching and training speakers and communicators, I've noticed that clients, in efforts to manage their precious time, have been dispensing with practice and preparation. Over the years, with business responsibilities growing for everyone, it has gotten much worse. When I suggest to my clients that for them to be very successful as communicators they will need hours of practice, they either look at me as if I am from another planet or they agree with my premise and still don't allot time to do the work. I think they have it in the backs of their minds that practice and rehearsal are only necessary for professional speakers.

However, when we dig a little deeper, they almost always come to the real-ization that, indeed, they need to work harder at preparing to communicate. They have noticed, for instance, that colleagues who do excel in communication get the plum assignments, promotions, and raises.

Therefore, in this section I would like to give you three pointers on practicing that will encourage you to use your valuable time efficiently and have you looking more professional and feeling more confident.

1. *Understand the practice-to-performing ratio.* It takes an average of 10 hours of practice for each hour of performance (10:1). This reality is terrifying to some people. However, if we consider all the things that we do every day that are part of the preparation process, such as self-talk (see below), the time expenditure becomes more acceptable and manageable. In addition, since every opportunity to communicate is a chance to become more familiar with how to say what you say, your need to practice will decrease. Of course, many things must be factored in. For example, a keynote speech requires much more and a very different type of preparation and rehearsal than a one-on-one meeting with a client or colleague.

2. *Talk to yourself.* You know all those people you see in their cars or walking down the street mumbling and talking to themselves? They're not bound for the insane asylum. They're practicing! Seriously, turn off your car radio or Walkman and use some of the moments you have in the car or alone to run through concepts, practice your introductory pitch, and rehearse telling stories and timing for jokes. I do it constantly while I'm walking down the street and during my daily bike ride. (And yes, I suffer relentless ribbing from my friends and family because of it.)

3. *Be systematic.* Instead of waiting until just before the communication opportunity takes place, plan a schedule that will give you enough time in advance to get ready. Again, how much time you spend depends on the nature of the communication. For informal communication, you should be looking at least a week ahead of the encounter. Every day, rehearse your introductory pitch or how you plan to greet the listener(s). This is also the time to consider what type of small talk you might make and compose a list of

questions you'd like to ask. This sounds like much more work than it is. It should only take a few minutes a day during that week in advance. And don't forget to jot down notes as you think of things so that you don't forget them. You can always discard those thoughts later or file them for later use.

Following is a practice schedule for different types of communication opportunities that will help you to chart your practice progress. Be mindful that many of the encounters must be planned further out than one week.

Pitch Practice Schedule

Type of meeting:

☐ Internal meeting
☐ Client meeting/sale
☐ Vendor meeting
☐ Phone conversation/conference call
☐ School-related meeting (board of education, PTA)
☐ Association get-together
☐ Convention or conference
☐ Workshop or seminar
☐ Speech or presentation
☐ Board meeting

Other important details:

_____

_____

_____

Date of meeting:_____

Reason for meeting:

☐ Sales call   ☐ Get information
☐ Client maintenance   ☐ Training
☐ Networking event

Other important details:

_____

_____

_____

Location:

☐ My office   ☐ Hotel
☐ Client's office   ☐ Conference center
☐ Vendor's office   ☐ School or municipal building
☐ Restaurant or other meal location   ☐ Private home

Room details:

_____

_____

Parties present:

Name/Position	Phone Number	E-Mail Address

Talking points:

_____

_____

_____

_____

(Use other side of sheet to add more, if necessary.)

Questions I want to ask:

_____

_____

_____

_____

_____

(Use other side of sheet to add more, if necessary.)

Goals for meeting:

☐ Get status report   ☐ Give status report
☐ Negotiation   ☐ Meet individual(s)
☐ Social/business   ☐ Sell product/service
☐ View facility   ☐ Deliver presentation

Other important details:

_____

_____

_____

Potential obstacles to achieving goals:

_____

_____

_____

(Use other side of sheet to add more, if necessary.)

Planning schedule:

- *Four weeks prior:*
  ☐ Make reservations.
  ☐ Schedule time to investigate meeting place.
  ☐ Do research, if necessary.

☐ Begin to jot down notes.
☐ Begin saying things out loud (includes talking to yourself).

Notes:

_____

_____

_____

- *Three weeks prior:*

  ☐ Investigate meeting place.
  ☐ Continue jotting down notes.
  ☐ Anticipate obstacles.
  ☐ Continue saying things out loud.
  ☐ View facility.

  Notes:

  _____

  _____

  _____

- *Two weeks prior:*

  ☐ Continue jotting down notes.
  ☐ Tweak notes.
  ☐ Continue saying things out loud.
  ☐ Consider solutions to obstacles.
  ☐ Begin to gather relevant materials.

  Notes:

  _____

  _____

  _____

- *One week prior:*

  ☐ Confirm reservation or meeting location details.
  ☐ Put finishing touches on notes.

☐ Tweak delivery.
☐ Make checklist of materials.
☐ Proof materials and put into finished form.
☐ Select wardrobe and check availability.
☐ Last-minute additions.

Notes:

_____

_____

_____

- *Two days prior:*
  ☐ Confirm meeting with attending parties.
  ☐ Proof materials again, just to be sure that everything is correct.
  ☐ Last-minute additions (only if absolutely necessary).
  ☐ Do quick run-throughs of important points.

  Notes:

  _____

  _____

  _____

- *Day before:*
  ☐ Lay things out so that you can walk out the door without forgetting anything.
  ☐ Using materials checklist, put things in carrying case.
  ☐ Resist urge to add anything more—too late and not necessary.
  ☐ Run through talking points.
  ☐ Relax—you're ready.

  Notes:

  _____

  _____

  _____

One more thing: Practicing is tedious and boring, which is another reason why many people don't do it. During the process, you can begin to feel as if your prospective listeners already know what you're going to say because *you* get so deeply into it. In fact, listeners will be hearing you for the first time, not the hundredth, which is the way it may feel to you, having gone over and over it. Take the long view—the more you practice, the better you'll become, and the practice-to-performing ratio will decrease. In addition, you'll have more time to go on that diet, get some exercise, be nicer to your kids, and so on.

GET COMFORTABLE WITH DISCOMFORT: THE INSIDE STORY ON STAGE FRIGHT

In my workshops and seminars I ask for a show of hands in response to the question, "How many of you feel nervous before you have to do a presentation?" Usually about three-quarters of the hands will shoot up. At that point I say, "Good. It's the rest of you I'm worried about." Discomfort or nervousness while communicating is part and parcel of the communication process. People often say to me, "I get so nervous when I meet someone for the first time or unexpectedly that I get tongue tied, and I feel like they can see me shaking all over." Well, in almost every case, the nervousness cannot be seen. People are surprised to know that even experienced communicators feel discomfort much of the time. The difference between them and the rest of the population is that they have learned to embrace the discomfort. What most people do instead is try to wish away the feelings of discomfort, hoping that eventually they'll disappear once and for all. This type of resistance exacerbates the fear because it never goes away entirely, nor should it. Great communicators have learned that the rush of adrenaline gives them an edge; it makes them more interesting and more on top of their game. They also know that this edge can occur only if they are well prepared. So here we are again, back to the twin themes of *practice* and *preparation*. These are the antidotes to the kind of nervousness and discomfort that can trip you up, make you stumble. If you practice the techniques outlined in this chapter, you may feel nervous, but you won't look it. In addition, the idea of faking it until you make it has a lot of merit because it can be a self-fulfilling prophecy.

Ruth's Truths for Chapter 12

Ruth's truth 63: Lack of preparation to communicate is a cardinal sin.

Ruth's truth 64: Stage fright goes with the territory.

Ruth's truth 65: Practice is the antidote to stage fright.

Persistence Persuades: The Vastly Neglected Art of Follow-up

Many of life's failures are people who did not realize how close they were to success when they gave up.

—Thomas Edison

Have you ever wondered how some people get ahead in life? I know that I have. These people succeed in careers that they seem to have marginal talent for. They exist in every business, every profession. So how do they do it? They are persistent. They are focused. They don't let setbacks derail their dreams. They never give up. And this stick-to-itiveness is incredibly persuasive. After a while, if you are still there, still pushing your wares, people begin to believe that you really are good, that you really can deliver, and you will get a chance to prove it. Now just imagine the heights someone who is persistent *and talented* could attain.

I happened to be meeting with members of the training department at an international investment bank the day after the stock market had taken a very serious plunge. The bank coincidentally had just finished rolling out a series of sales training programs for investment bankers. During our meeting, the training managers began to get feedback on a key portion of the program—following up with clients when there is good news *and bad*. Now they were facing some very bad news.

In the past the bankers would wait for clients to contact them. The clients usually would be upset, many yelling and making gratuitous comments, so you can imagine the trepidation of the bankers at the prospect of taking the initiative to contact these angry clients first, portfolio managers who were holding stocks and funds the bankers had recommended and sold to them—stocks and funds that had lost a significant portion of their value in just a few short hours. Calling clients now felt like asking for trouble. The temptation was very strong to hold off on making first contact to follow up. Things were bad enough without pouring salt on this wound. Why should they set themselves up for a further fall?

Well, some of the bankers who had gone through the sales training program overcame their fear and picked up the phone to make the calls. The result? Gratitude. Yes, that's right, *gratitude,* for having had the guts to call and see how their clients were feeling, discuss the reasons it might have happened, and just plain commiserate. These portfolio managers, not known for being faint of heart, were consoled by the simple gesture of a phone call meant to reach out to them and help them buck up during a time of great stress. Oh, and they told these bankers that they were the only ones who had called. Guess which investment bank got the next piece of business?

WHAT IS FOLLOW-UP?

Follow-up is a process by which you make contact with someone to reinforce and further an end. For instance, if I have just met with a client, I would follow up with a thank-you note or a letter that summarized the conversation and thanked the client for his time. Another type of follow-up is calling a friend who may be ill or sending flowers to a loved one to celebrate something. Following up is a lost art. It is so lost and so rare that people can stand out merely by doing it. Following up serves the following purposes:

- It lets people know you care.
- It identifies you as responsible for the process.
- It keeps relationships alive and invigorated.
- It provides opportunities for new interactions.
- It plants seeds for new ideas.
- It shows a high level of commitment.
- It demonstrates self-confidence.

The bankers achieved all these purposes. They

- *Let someone know they cared.* They put themselves in the shoes of their clients and reached out in a time of great stress and worry.
- *Identified themselves as responsible parties.* They respectfully accepted their part in the drama and did not shy away from bad news.
- *Kept the relationships alive and invigorated.* They dealt with some sharp exchanges that naturally would exist in such situations.
- *Provided opportunities for new interactions.* They discussed potential solutions to the problems and strategies to avoid them in the future.
- *Planted seeds for new ideas.* Both parties came away thinking creatively.
- *Showed a high level of commitment.* They did not allow the debacle to deter them.
- *Demonstrated self-confidence.* They did not let their fear inform their behavior.

The result of those single, individual calls was enormous prestige bestowed on the investment bankers and their employer—just the opposite of what those who didn't call received.

Follow-up takes organization because you have to keep records. Today there is an enormous selection of contact management systems ranging from paper planners to software that does an outstanding job of keeping records, reminding users of appointments, and scheduling follow-up contact.

There also has been the advent of the personal digital assistant (PDA). Such devices are equipped to synchronize data with computers, keeping everyone's calendars up to date. In several places in this book I mention the love-hate relationship that I have with technology. In this case I have fallen head-over-heels in love. In addition to the convenience of data synchronization, I like the compact size of my PDA. The technology now also exists to synchronize over the Web. Thus, if you are traveling, you can log on, plug in, and update your information instantly. If you have postponed buying a PDA or are daunted by the prospect of transcribing and entering all the information, I can empathize. But I urge you to take the plunge, get the data-entry out of the way (hire a high school student to do it for you), and breathe easy knowing how much time you will be saving from now on.

Earlier I mentioned the idea of sending a thank-you to someone who has done something nice for you, such as referring you to a potential client or hosting an event that you enjoyed. With the advent of e-mail, handwritten notes have become a thing of the past. But I love them. I love sending them, and I love receiving them. Writing a handwritten note takes just a little more work than sending an e-mail and is well worth the trouble. I keep boxes of blank cards available, usually of great artists. Some people have cards with their business logos or names printed on them. These are good too. A further touch is to use a nice stamp. The U.S. Postal Service maintains a variety of beautiful stamps for sale, and new ones become available regularly. They cost the same as the others and add flair. It's surprising how much people take away from these small tokens. They show that you are willing to reveal a little of your personality, as well as being a very effective way of letting people know that you care.

TOO MUCH OR TOO LITTLE? THE FINE LINE BETWEEN FOLLOWING UP AND PESTERING

One Saturday morning at about 8:00 the phone rang. It was a telemarketer. I am always polite but direct, and I asked this fellow if he seriously expected me to buy something from someone disturbing me at my home at a time I should be relaxing, quite possibly even sleeping? He didn't miss a beat, going on to say how difficult it had been to reach me. Well, yeah! At that point, I let my irritation show and told him that that was not a good excuse for calling me at such a time and that I would not be buying anything either then or in the future from the company he was representing. I used measured tones, but my message was clear. Pessimist that I am, I'm sure he'll call again soon, but it's nice to dream. Another incident occurred when a telemarketer who had apparently spoken to my husband and gotten some kind of commitment to donate from him that I did not know about called to remind him. Since my husband was on a two-week business trip, I told the marketer that nothing would be done until his return. At that point the rep began to badger and scold me, saying things about promises not kept and so forth. Again, I politely cut him off, admonished him not to scold me, and repeated that it would be two weeks before he would have an answer.

As you may be thinking, these telemarketers demonstrated unacceptable ways to follow up. While no one should ever make commitments they have no intention of keeping, people don't make good on promises for many reasons. The biggest reason is lack of time to consider the offer. Another is the proliferation of junk mail. I throw out three-quarters of the paper mail I receive. There are so many fires to put out and so many unexpected crises that arise in personal and business lives that a person may have to make many attempts to follow up before making headway in the communication. In my own business, I have known many instances where I followed up periodically for several years before getting any business. This is not unusual and is a example of how *persistence persuades.* People derive meaning from tenacity and determination. This behavior conveys to them that you will be just as dogged and unshakable in work they may be paying you for, perhaps even more so.

There is a very fine line between following up and pestering, and it's important to know where one ends and the other begins. A great deal depends on the relationship, the type of situation, the urgency, and the agreement you have with the follow-up party. When I am calling clients, I always ask them when a good time to follow up would be. The responses vary, but merely asking identifies me as taking charge. They can relax because they know I consider it part of my job. If I'm prospecting by making cold calls, the follow-up sequence usually ranges from one to six months, depending on the time of year, budgets, fiscal year, and other considerations. Some clients insist that they have no need for services and do not anticipate ever having a need. In those cases I ask if it's all right if I put them on my mailing list so that I can send them articles I may have seen or keep them abreast of what I've been doing. I can count on one hand the number of times people have said no. So with that group the follow-up takes on a different look, but it is still follow up. By the way, for the few who do say no, they should be respected, and no further contact should take place.

If a client is not available when I call or when I can't get past the secretary and I decide to leave a voice message (rather than calling until I reach the person), my voice mail is very carefully done. I usually write it out on a little program I have called "Stickies" that resembles Post-it notes:

1. *I state my name:* "Hi Charlie, this is Ruth Sherman at Ruth Sherman Associates."
2. *I mention when we last spoke and what we discussed:* "We spoke about two months ago regarding some media training for some of your senior managers."
3. *I remind the person of our agreement regarding follow-up:* "And you asked me to give you a call around mid-September."
4. *I leave my name and number, invite them to call me, and set a new follow-up date:* "Please give me a call if you're ready to discuss the media training. If I don't hear from you, I'll give you a call next month. Thanks, Charlie. Bye."

Then I immediately enter the details on my desktop or PDA and set an alarm to remind me to follow up as I had promised. I also might use that last point to give myself a plug, such as mentioning a new client I am doing similar work for or inviting the prospect to a presentation I'm giving.

Notice that I used the word *promise* above. I use that particular word because it inspires me to keep it. Keeping promises is a wonderful way to leave clients and others with a good impression. Again, it is something that they can take away and project onto any future business they may do with you.

I have had clients tell me that the way I follow up is the best they have ever experienced and that they appreciate it and don't feel pestered or manipulated. This is gratifying to me because it takes so much effort and discipline. None of what is covered in this book can be accomplished without persistence. Persistence requires following up and following through. Persistence opens doors and allows for exploration and discovery. Persistence requires a fairly unshakable belief that you are on the right path and the ability to not be put off by the inevitable setbacks. The art of follow-up should be honed by anyone who wants to have a greater impact in her business and professional life. The fact that it is so vastly neglected makes this an excellent factor to help you stand out from the crowd.

Ruth's Truths for Chapter 13

Ruth's truth 66: Countless opportunities are lost because of lack of follow-up.

Ruth's truth 67: Have the courage to face people when delivering bad news.

Ruth's truth 68: Use a PDA and contact management software to keep track of follow-up activities.

Ruth's truth 69: Write personal, handwritten thank-you notes on unique cards and use a nice stamp.

Ruth's truth 70: There is a fine line between following up and pestering. Read the situation, and don't be a pest.

The Likability Factor

At the beginning of the book, in Chapter 1, I mentioned that to be a successful communicator, you have to like people. Conversely, people have to like you back. So what makes for likability? Why is it important? Don't a lot of people get ahead who are not likable? It's difficult to give definitive answers here. Different characteristics appeal to different people. For example, we all have friends whose significant others we wonder about. Somehow we settle on the reality of "different strokes for different folks." Still, to be likable, I believe that the usual traits apply: kindness, generosity, magnanimity, politeness, keeping your word, and so on.

Being likable for most people is important because, as with other types of communication issues, it can act as a differentiator. Maintaining this quality helps you to stand out from the crowd, not to mention being gratifying to both sender and receiver. Approachable and go-to people are appealing to almost everyone. Those who go out of their way to help others are perceived as being able to get the job done. Then there are those who work hard and go the extra mile, but often they do it with a scowl or while complaining loudly. There is a great deal to be said for being pleasant and cooperative. I'm a stickler for being nice. The old saying about attracting more bees with honey is true

There are, as indicated above, plenty of people who get ahead without seeming likable. The operative word in the previous sentence is *seeming*. I suspect that these folks have an ability to develop specific, targeted relationships that help them to succeed. So while they may not be generally well liked, they have been able to cultivate strategic relationships that work in their favor. I remember, as a naïve, young professional, just out of college, being astounded by the rudeness and just plain mean-spiritedness I encountered in some of my first jobs. I wondered repeatedly how certain people had managed to get ahead. As I've matured, my view is far less clouded by youthful idealism. Not everyone needs to be likable to succeed. But most people do.

A law firm called on me to work with one of its young associates whom I'll call Benjamin. As usual, the firm thought Benjamin was very smart and capable. However, he was having trouble connecting with others, and this posed a problem. The firm's managers thought that it had something to do with the fact that he was not a native of the United States. They thought that perhaps there were some cultural obstacles, a logical conclusion. We planned to meet once a week and see what strategies we could put in place to help Benjamin be more successful relating to his coworkers.

It became clear early on that Benjamin didn't want to attend our meetings. He never brought anything to discuss, and he never seemed to give our meetings much thought or try any of the strategies I suggested. He responded to all my questions with one-word or very brief answers. Every time I came up with an idea, he would reject it. He placed numerous, impossible barriers between us. In these types of situations, there is not much I can do. I depend on my coaching clients to reflect on the concepts that we discuss and get into the habit of working these concepts into their everyday thinking. I tell them that they must bring situations, experiences, and questions they have to my attention so that we can analyze them and flesh them out. I serve as a reflection, feeding back, giving my impressions, and asking probing questions designed to get them to think, unearth new ideas, identify threads in their communicative behaviors, and draw parallels between the way they communicate and the results they get. Their responsibility is to make a good effort at introspection; if they aren't willing to be introspective, the coaching relationship is starved and cannot succeed.

After a few meetings, I mentioned to Benjamin that I was feeling frustrated and that I felt that he was blocking any progress. When I asked him what he thought, he blurted out that he didn't understand why he had been sent to me in the first place, that other people didn't have to go, that he wasn't having any trouble, and that he didn't know why he had to become a better communicator. After all, he did his work diligently, and people seemed satisfied with his output. It was a case of *"The work speaks for itself"* and nothing else should matter (see Chapter 4). I was relieved that he at last let me know how he was feeling. I very gently told him that although much of what he said was true and that he was certainly an intelligent person, unless he was precociously gifted or fit into the genius category and had come up with solutions to problems no one had ever thought of before, he would have to begin to build relationships with more of his colleagues to be successful. He would have to grease the wheels a bit. I told him that I had been brought in because people were feeling uncomfortable around him and couldn't seem to make inroads and that, interestingly, I was experiencing something similar and that the beauty of coaching is that it often mirrors what is actually going on. Unfortunately, Benjamin didn't buy it, so I told him that I thought it would be best if we discontinued our meetings. The last I heard, Benjamin had left the firm.

Getting along, employing behaviors that increase likability, and working to convey to others that you like them make it much easier for you to navigate the rough seas of the business and social environments.

MANNERS MATTER

A key element of being likable is good manners. The world is a very competitive place, so it should come as no surprise that people should use any and all advantages possible. Having impeccable manners and understanding the rules of etiquette are critical determinants of success and key to winning people over. I do not know a single highly successful person who does not have these skills down to a science. Unfortunately, the boundaries of propriety have been eroding steadily over the past two or three decades. In fact, I have noticed an acceleration of this trend as technology has gotten more sophisticated. I think the reason is that as productivity has been increased via automation, people aren't talking to or seeing each other as much and they've grown rusty on interpersonal skills. The following examples may ring a bell:

- An executive who regularly returns from lunch with food spattered on his tie
- A passenger on a commuter train who is speaking very loudly on his cell phone

- An executive who walks in 20 minutes late for a lunch meeting and sits down without a word of acknowledgment or apology
- The host of a social event who spends a disproportionate amount of time speaking to a couple of guests, virtually ignoring the other people he invited
- Audience members who talk or let their cell phones and pagers ring during a theatrical performance
- Drivers who come speeding up the right shoulder to gain a couple of seconds on those who remain in lane to wait their turn and exit safely
- The telemarketer who speaks nonstop, ignores entreaties or objections, and who won't take no for an answer
- The pedestrian who steps a few yards in front of you to be in a more advantageous position to flag down a taxi

These examples are just a very few of the hundreds, if not thousands, of incidents of rude and obnoxious behavior that occur daily and that negatively affect our quality of life. And it could be viewed as a sad commentary on the current state of affairs that I would even suggest being courteous and mannerly as something that can differentiate one person from another. But, hey, it's a fact of life, so let's roll with it.

Good manners are skills in which the lessons are best begun early in childhood. My husband and I have been on a good manners crusade for years with our children. We often tease our teenage daughter about her table manners. The teasing usually takes place after a particularly egregious faux pas such as licking her plate or eating with her nose practically in her food so that she can shovel it in or just vacuum up a particularly tasty morsel. We create imaginary scenarios to help us illustrate the potential consequences of poor manners. One concerns a dinner with Bill Gates as part of the interview process for a big job at Microsoft. In the imaginary scenario, she exhibits less than exemplary table manners, and after the dinner, Gates tells her, "Sorry, we chose the person who didn't lick the plate." As we expect, she is contemptuous of this type of ribbing. Still, a recent indicator of our success is that she just told us about one of her friends whom she noticed chewing with her mouth open and how disgusting it was. Of course, it never occurred to me that teaching manners to our children would be such a protracted process. Recently, we've begun to get serious with our ten-year-old. Unfortunately, most people aren't taught well, if at all, don't learn what they need to, and end up paying an unnecessarily high price.

There are a great many reasons for having good manners, but if you want just one, it is that it bespeaks good breeding. In some circles it also represents higher social rank or class. And this is the case regardless of your actual background. Access to these skills is free and available to anyone with the desire and a library card or an Internet connection. Whatever one's background or level of wealth, today's competitive world absolutely demands good manners.

My friend and colleague, Diane Gargiulo, is a fabulous example of that combined one-two-three punch—expertise, niceness, and impeccable manners. When people talk about Diane, they always point to how nice she is. Every time I am with her, I feel like I am the smartest, most interesting, funniest individual on the planet. I marvel at her party-giving skills. As a host, she has few peers. Everything, from her creative invitations, to a party's theme and location, to the inventive and delicious food and drinks, is designed to welcome guests into her world and to make them feel good. I vividly recall being invited to her London apartment during an overseas assignment. She served cocktails and set out little plates of delicious olives and candied nuts. These were small but highly effective gestures. Diane makes this kind of thing look effortless, but as anyone who has ever had people to their home knows, it's far from easy. Although she has never said so, I imagine that she must be exhausted after one of her soirees, but like all successful communicating, it is also energizing.

Another responsibility of the host that Diane does very well is to help her guests meet each other and mingle. The minute a guest walks into Diane's space, she is there, greeting, taking their coat, offering them a drink, and ushering them into a conversation. It is as if she has looked at her guest list beforehand and decided who should meet whom. And it wouldn't surprise me at all if that were exactly what she does. Finally, it is important to distinguish that although Diane is the real deal, genuinely nice and thoughtful, she understands very well the benefits that accrue to her through the display of such social graces. She knows that making people feel comfortable is a quality that will keep her fondly in people's memories; they will look for opportunities to be around her, to socialize with her, and to do business with her.

I just received an invitation to an event Diane is giving, and I am excited to go. I know that I'll have a good time, eat some good food, and meet some very interesting people. Diane is the epitome of charm and class.

CELL DAMAGE: REGULATING YOUR USE OF MOBILE TECHNOLOGY

We are more connected than ever, and as Neil Postman, the late, great media and technology critic and one of my graduate school professors, asserted repeatedly, technology is a double-edged sword: It gives something, and it takes something away. The biggest problem I have with our newfound connectedness is the intrusion on what used to be considered quiet, private, or personal time. I refer to calls that come in to my phone, as well as those that others take and make. The phones ring everywhere, all the time. I was at a high school performance of *Romeo and Juliet* just this past weekend, and during the last dramatic scene, not one but three phones rang!

In addition to the ringing, due to the problem of widespread poor reception—not to mention the noise inherent in public spaces—we have to speak loudly to be heard. It's very distracting and very inconsiderate. It is another way our norms of propriety have been eroded. I am always annoyed when others invade my quiet time. When my own phone rings, I ask the caller to wait until I can walk to a location that offers some privacy or tell the caller I will call back when I have a moment to myself. It always makes me self-conscious and uncomfortable and is one reason that I have made a personal decision not to indiscriminately give out my cell phone number. I find the whole idea that I or anyone else should make themselves constantly available to be presumptuous and a pretext for rude, intrusive behavior. And there's the rub: Why is it that so many things that used to be able to wait no longer can? Patience is no longer a virtue, and with this loss, the courtesy threshold has been lowered substantially.

Before I become too preachy, I will acknowledge that the battle has been all but lost. Being a persistent optimist, though, I believe the fight for good manners can be joined on other fronts. As you navigate the interpersonal communication landscape and strive to make a good impression in a short amount of time, keep in mind the following:

1. *Use good table manners.*
2. *Be prudent with alcohol.*
3. *Send handwritten thank-you notes.* When a thank-you or other personal sentiment is called for, write your note by hand. This never fails to leave a good impression (see Chapter 13 for more on note writing).
4. *Accept a business card with interest.* When it is proffered, take it, look at it, and comment on some aspect of it (design, color, information, position of the giver). Don't just shove it into your pocket or purse.
5. *Regulate cell phone use.* During meetings, if possible, turn off your phone. At the very least, set it to vibrate instead of ring. If you are expecting an important call that you must take, forewarn your companions and apologize in advance. When the call does come in, politely excuse yourself and find a more private spot. In public places where you must be on the phone, speak quietly. In places where you are confined with others, such as public transportation, do not take calls unless it is absolutely necessary, and then either speak quietly or explain your situation to the other person and politely ask if you can call her at a more convenient time. Be very careful of speaking about confidential information in a place where others are likely to hear.
6. *Be polite.* Say "Please," "Thank you," "May I," and other similar words and phrases to let people know when you have gratitude or would like permission. Your mother was right about this.
7. *Keep promises.* This is self-explanatory, but if you can't keep a promise, an explanation is required.
8. *Maintain confidences.* Not only may you risk your career by divulging proprietary information, but also no one likes a person who can't keep a secret.

Finally, it is important to keep in mind that people throughout the world do not follow the same rules and conventions that we do in this country. Actions that would not be considered rude here may be the ultimate slap in the face in China or the Middle East. If you are planning a trip abroad for business or pleasure, learn about the protocol and what is considered acceptable behavior before you go. Don't assume that because a country may be a part of the West or is English-speaking, it has the same rules of protocol as we do here. Moreover, local customs in this country, while not as starkly different, can vary from region to region. The important thing is to be prepared—again.

There is much more to know about having good manners, and I suggest learning as much as possible. A good rule of thumb is to take your cues from people in your world who are highly successful. There are also numerous books and Web sites on etiquette that spell things out in very accessible ways. Having good manners, like conversational rituals, act as smoothers, leave wonderful lasting impressions, and keep things pleasantly and positively moving forward.

Ruth's Truths for Chapter 14

Ruth's truth 71: Not only is it important to like people, but it's also important to be liked.

Ruth's truth 72: Impeccable manners will make you a standout.

Ruth's truth 73: Regulate how you use your cell phone.

Ruth's truth 74: Be polite.

Ruth's truth 75: Keep promises.

Ruth's truth 76: Maintain confidences.

Provide Good Phone and E-Mail

By now you know that I believe that face-to-face contact with others is king. But there is also a place for other types of communicating, namely, telephone and e-mail.

We are more connected than ever, and as Neil Postman, who researched and commented extensively and brilliantly on the effects of technology on our lives, found, the outcome isn't always positive regardless of what the technology gurus would like us to believe.

Now that e-mail and voice mail have been around awhile, you'd think we would have mastered the art of using them to greatest advantage. This has not been the case, I'm sad to report. Many aspects of each of these technologies have created new challenges for an already overworked population. Three in particular stand out:

- E-mail and/or voice-mail overload
- Poor message quality
- Clutter

The first, *overload*, continues to worsen and poses problems that lately have become worthy of governmental involvement. Before the junk e-mail onslaught, it had been commonplace for many business executives to receive 100 to 200 messages in a single day. Now that number easily can be doubled or tripled. So-called spam has morphed into being a primary time waster and cost factor for many businesses. Even without the spam, the more senior you are and the higher your level in the organization, the more messages you will receive. Because senior executives' time is more expensive, the cost to the company is greater.

The second problem, *poor message quality*, is something I covered earlier in this book (see Chapter 7), although not in relation to e-mail. Because e-mail communication has evolved to be much less formal than other types of business writing, users have dispensed with the formality of planning, in addition to spelling and grammar. Poorly planned messages are poorly aimed and do not hit their targets or meet their goals of communicating information.

The third problem, *clutter*, is related to overload. Important or urgent messages share the increasingly crowded stage with unnecessary or irrelevant messages. The critical messages thus can be ignored or deleted inadvertently.

The ubiquity of e-mail has caused some unintended problems as well. In addition to presentation and communication skills, I also help nonnative speakers of English to become more fluent by teaching them to reduce their accents. As with other communication skills, these clients must practice their skills, especially English conversation. It is the principal way they can assess whether they've become more comprehensible. Ten years ago, even though e-mail had hit its stride and was well in use, people didn't use it for everything and spent far more time in direct speech communication. Today, a client of mine who is a young lawyer and whose firm wants him to improve his speaking skills tells me that he engages in English conversation less than 10 hours per week. I find this very disturbing. While he spends much time drilling, also part of the practice routine, there is no way for him to improve as rapidly as he would if he had more chances to practice the actual skills. My clients of 10 years ago and earlier were much more successful because of the abundant opportunities to practice their skills.

In the early days of e-mail and voice mail, companies provided training and/or guidelines to instruct employees when it was appropriate to send messages. E-mail was necessary only if it was impossible or impractical to telephone or meet face to face. Today, we e-mail people occupying offices right next door.

Part of the problem is that e-mail has become a way to *avoid* face-to-face meetings. Sometimes this strategy makes sense, such as when a face-to-face meeting would be too time-consuming or when it would be appropriate to allow tensions to cool down. More often than not, however, a face-to-face meeting or a direct telephone conversation is a more effective solution.

Choosing the appropriate medium for communication can be interpreted as evidence of leadership qualities because it indicates a willingness to take responsibility for the communication. Many people choose instead to *avoid* or *shift* responsibility.

A critically important thing to remember about workplace e-mail and voice mail is that any information transmitted via these technologies becomes the property of the company that owns them. Recent news items have made it all too clear that records of these communications are saved and can be retrieved, often years later for the purposes of investigations.[1]

Aside from personal breaches such as those just described, be careful to protect other people's confidentiality. Once confidential information is sent through e-mail or voice mail, it is no longer confidential. And the existence of passwords to access personal voice-mail or e-mail boxes is no guarantee of protection. Anyone may be able to access your mailboxes. Someone may be walking by your desk and glance at an e-mail that is either on your screen or has been printed out. Anything that can be classified as confidential should *not* be transmitted via e-mail or voice mail. These media are *not secure.*

E-mail address books, while convenient, also make us more prone to mistakes. Recently, I sent a detailed e-mail concerning a client to his supervisor, Nancy. Because I had her address in my e-mail address book, I only had to type the first few letters of her name. Of the list of Nancys that appeared, I clicked on one and pressed send. To my dismay, I immediately realized that I had sent the message to the wrong Nancy, which meant that information about this client was sent to someone else. Fortunately, being aware of these types of problems, I never use clients' names in such e-mails but refer to them in other ways. I had to resend the e-mail and also send a follow-up e-mail to the person who mistakenly received the first one to explain my mistake. It was embarrassing and may have an impact on my getting business from the mistaken recipient; as a result of my error, she could be thinking that I cannot be trusted with confidential information.

E-MAIL

As I mentioned earlier, e-mail has developed a reputation for being less formal than other written business communication, and its level of formality keeps declining. Basically, it has become a substitute for speaking. People don't seem to worry about spelling, so typos abound. Grammar suffers as well, and whatever happened to capitalization? Many e-mails I receive look like they might have been written by e. e. cummings, the poet whose trademark is no capitalization. Still, poor spelling and grammar, though seemingly much more widely accepted in e-mail, can have consequences, so some care is indicated. Higher-level executives have more latitude. This is so because they have already proved themselves and have been promoted accordingly. However, if you are a junior to midlevel executive, it is better to err on the side of caution when it comes to spelling and grammar. And if you're in business for yourself, like I am, don't take a chance. I think of e-mail as being somewhere between being a substitute for speaking and a replacement for letter writing. And importantly, e-mails with proper grammar and spelling are easier to read and allow for quicker understanding. Use spell and grammar checkers if you have them, but be aware that these programs don't check for context. The word *public* can easily be typed as *pubic* and will not be picked up by a spell checker. I'll never forget the e-mail I got from a vendor who wrote of the "eternal" meeting when he meant to say *external.* Avoid embarrassing incidents by proofreading as much as possible. By the way, this is another good reason to keep messages short. It is much easier to quickly proofread a short, well-organized message than a long and complicated one. If you are going to print out an e-mail to use as a memo, it essentially becomes a more formal, written business document requiring a greater degree of attention to grammar and spelling. Therefore, check the memo before distributing it. Remember, you never know who may see it.

People are working so hard these days that they skim e-mails and often miss important parts. This creates more work for everyone because the person who sent it does not receive a full response and must then resend the part of the message that didn't get through the first time. The receiver must then answer again. A client told me about a situation in which this happened recently. His message asked three questions. When he got the reply, only one was answered, so he had to resend the other two. The next reply answered one more question. This left a third question still unanswered. He held off resending the third part because clearly the recipient was too busy at that moment to give my client's e-mail the time it requires. Being sensitive to these waves of busyness is crucial to knowing how to proceed and getting expectations met. It occurs to me that this back and forth has been a time waster. Therefore, if you are the sender, do your best to assess the situation of the receiver so that you can accommodate that person's capacity for responding at a certain level of detail. If you are on the receiving end, before responding to messages, try to read the entire message. If you don't have time, save it so that you can review it when you do have time. Do a quick reply to the sender saying so. It will save you time in the long run. Finally, though I love e-mail, direct phone contact is a much more efficient use of time. I've had many an occasion when I've gone back and forth e-mailing someone over the course of a couple of hours only to get frustrated, pick up the phone, and complete the communication in a couple of minutes.

Temper Your 'Tude

I know that I have said that speech is mostly nonverbal and writing is mostly verbal, but in the case of e-mail, innovative human beings have found ways to inject attitude into their e-mails. Sometimes referred to as *flaming,* the sender of an e-mail message typically uses graphic and linguistic devices to communicate negative or angry feelings. It is the same as if the person were shouting. I can't say this strongly enough: *This is completely inappropriate and unsuitable* and can be very damaging if used in a business setting. While certain feelings can be stated directly in e-mails, highly charged emotional states should never be communicated either electronically or in other writing. It's unprofessional at the very least, and at most, it's a hard, permanent record of a momentary outburst that could be held against you. Whereas some emotions contained in speech can be denied, there's no getting around it when it's written down. When in doubt, remember that as in face-to-face communication, the less emotion used, the better. As a highly emotional person, I have to remind myself of this constantly. At times when I would like to lash out, I must force myself to take a step back and reposition my communication approach.

"That's Not Funny!" Jokes and Humor Can Backfire

Jokes and humor are other areas where great care needs to be taken. There is a real danger of offending someone with a joke they may not find funny. In addition, in my own experience, it's akin to getting more junk mail. While I think I have a pretty good sense of humor and love a good joke or funny story, I have been put off by having to wade through all the forwarding information. By the time I make it to the punch line, I often find that the payoff is not that funny, so my time and effort have been wasted. I hated to do it, but I've had to ask family members to stop forwarding every silly story and joke they receive. My husband, who has the best sense of humor of anyone I know, has been appalled at some of the poor judgment people in his business sphere have used when choosing jokes and humor to disseminate over e-mail. And if this isn't enough to discourage you, businesses have taken a very dim view of these types of communications and a hard line against offenders. Oh, and remember that if people send you unsuitable things, you need to shut them down as soon as possible. Employers don't often distinguish between those on the sending or receiving ends of such communiqués. The bottom line: Sending or receiving an unsuitable e-mail reflects poorly on you.

Tune in to Tone

The tone or tenor of your communication is very important. If you are feeling impatient, be aware that it may come across in your e-mail messages. If you receive a message whose tone is questionable, step back from it first. Don't automatically assume that you are being personally attacked. Some people just write in a brusque, no-frills way. Give the benefit of the doubt, and don't respond in kind.

VOICE MAIL

Answering machines have been around for decades, so I continue to be astonished that people still don't use them or their digital counterpart, voice mail, to greatest effectiveness. One of the biggest obstacles for many people is recording the outgoing message. This is the greeting that you record on your voice-mail system or on your answering machine that too often ends with, "At the sound of the tone, please leave your message" or something similar. We also repeatedly hear, "I'm either on the phone or away from my desk." The reason we hear these same outgoing messages on so many voice-mail systems or machines is that the voice-mail companies provide scripts of messages that subscribers can use, and these messages are the same for everyone.

Be More Outgoing

Think about it: An outgoing message represents you. It is your public voice, and therefore, it makes sense to control the message it sends both verbally and nonverbally. I consider an outgoing message to be so important that I often have to record it several times before I'm happy with the result (which is probably the reason for the show business saying, "Never be your own producer."). I am very picky. I know that my outgoing message is a chance to make or cement a good first impression (see Chapter 1), so I want it to sound just right.

Because we tend to write our message down before we read it aloud for recording, it *sounds* written. Written speech is devoid of nonverbal considerations. A typical outgoing message from an office sounds like this:

Hello. You have reached the voice mailbox of John Jones. I am currently unavailable to speak to you. Please leave your name and number at the sound of the tone, and I will return your call as soon as possible. Thank you for calling. BEEEEEEP!

The tone of the language is stilted and does not allow for much warmth or expression. Note that there are no contractions and that he uses the words *currently unavailable,* which he likely would not have used in everyday conversation. Now look at this message as revised to sound more conversational:

Hi, this is John Jones. I'm sorry I can't speak to you personally at the moment but would like to return your call. Please leave a message, and I'll get back to you as soon as I can. Thanks, and talk to you soon. BEEEEP!

The revision uses language that is much more typical of conversation and has a more relaxed, welcoming tone. If you are struggling with how to structure your outgoing message, think about how you would speak it. An important issue to consider is word choice. Use the less formal versions of words:

ask instead of *request*
not here instead of *unavailable*
can't instead of *unable to*
thanks instead of *thank you*

Remember, too, that it's okay to use contractions.

I strive to meet the following goals whenever I record an outgoing voice message.

Voice	Vocal tone should convey warmth, be welcoming, appropriately upbeat, and polite.
Diction	Precise, clear, and crisp; words should be easy to understand; caller should not have to call back to hear the message a second time to absorb everything.
Rate	Moderate; tendency is to speak too quickly, so the speaker should consciously slow it down.
Content	*Business:* First and last names, business area or department, if necessary, so caller knows if she is in the right place; plans for returning call. If name is unfamiliar to average person or difficult to spell, take care to say it slowly and deliberately. Spelling it out is not necessary because there are other ways the caller can acquire this information. Nonnative speakers of English may need to add extra care. Thank person for calling.
	Personal: First or last names (this is a matter of personal preference), request for message and intention to return call. Thank person for calling.

Incoming Traffic

We also have to leave messages on others' machines and voice-mail systems. One of the things we can do to help ourselves is to prepare to leave messages. I'm always calling clients and other business contacts. Because these people are very busy, I'm accustomed to leaving messages in their voice mailboxes, so that's what I prepare for. I tend to not be very smooth off the cuff, so I try to plan a bit. Here again I use "Stickies," the tiny program that imitates Post-it notes and can be called up and saved at a moment's notice. I love them. So I summon a "Sticky" and write out what I plan to say, word for word. That's right, I write every word of the message I am going to leave so that I can read it verbatim. Now please keep in mind that I have become very skilled at writing for the ear.[2] I know how it is supposed to sound to someone who is listening. So be careful if you decide to write out your message.

Because I want to get my point across quickly and concisely, I also use *SALES* (see Chapter 7). A sample message is broken down as follows:

S*tate the main message.* "Hi Carlos, it's Ruth Sherman. Hope you're doing well. I'm calling to set up some time to meet with you next week."

A*dd key points.* "This is in addition to the July workshop you participated in. After that workshop, I suggested to Linda that I meet with you and a couple of the others privately."

L*ist benefits.* "The reason for this is there are things we can do in a private, one-on-one meeting that we can't do as well in the group setting."

E*xamples.* "For example, we can discuss issues that are particular to your situation. This is something I try to do in all my workshops because of how well it works at addressing individual concerns."

S*ummarize/specify next steps.* "I have some openings next Wednesday or Thursday, October 12 or 13, in the morning for about 30 to 45 minutes. Call or e-mail me and let me know if either of those days works for you and what time would be good. My phone number is [add number], and my e-mail is [add address]. Thanks, Carlos. Look forward to hearing back from you. Bye."

This is how it looked:

> Hi Carlos, it's Ruth Sherman. Hope you're doing well. I'm calling to set up some time to meet with you next week.
>
> This is an addition to the workshop you participated in in July. After that workshop, I suggested to Linda that I meet with you and a couple of the others privately.
>
> The reason for this is there are things we can do in a private, one-on-one meeting, that we can't do as well in the group setting.
>
> This is something I try to do in all my workshops because of how well it works at addressing individual concerns.
>
> I have some openings next Wednesday or Thursday, October 12 or 13, in the morning for about 30-45 minutes. Call or e-mail me and let me know if either of those days works for you and what time would be good. My phone number is ——————— and my e-mail is ———————.
>
> Thanks Carlos. I look forward to hearing back from you. Bye.

The important thing to notice here is the casual, conversational style of my writing. The tone of my language is warm and carefully designed not to cause any anxiety. The tone of my voice was correspondingly informal. More specifically, I used contractions and didn't use any big words or technical jargon. The message took less than a minute to deliver.

Now I'd like to demonstrate how it might sound if I had written it for the eye:

State the main message. "Carlos, This is Ruth Sherman. I hope everything is going well for you. I am calling because I would like schedule an appointment to meet with you next week."

Add key points. "This meeting is an addendum to the workshop in which you were a participant during the month of July. At the conclusion of that workshop, I met with Linda and suggested to her that I meet with you and two of the other participants privately."

List benefits. "I have found over the years that there are things we can do in a private, one-on-one meeting that are less likely to be accomplished when group dynamics are involved."

Examples. "A good example is that we can address concerns that are specific to your situation. I always attempt to meet privately with workshop clients because it is so effective at cementing some of the learning that takes place during the workshop itself and adds value."

Summarize/specify next steps. "I have some openings next Wednesday or Thursday, October 12 or 13, in the morning for about 30 to 45 minutes. Contact me at your earliest convenience to schedule an appointment. My phone and e-mail information are [add phone number and e-mail address]. I look forward to hearing from you and seeing you soon. Thank you."

This example is not nearly as friendly and warm as the first version. My language is much more formal and precise. I have tried to be grammatically correct and have used a few technical terms and unique-to-my-field jargon that I don't use in my conversational speech. It took well over a minute to deliver. I could soften it with my vocal tone, but the combination of both appropriate verbal tone and vocal tone will have a much better effect.

Voice mail is ubiquitous, and nothing irritates busy people more than incoherent or meandering messages. And we're all familiar with the poor soul who needs to call back again to finish the message he or she couldn't finish in two whole minutes. A few years ago a client of mine, an executive at a major music and entertainment company, told me about the following voice-mail exchange that took place between two of her employees.

Message: "The VP will be in on Monday and Tuesday. She'd like to meet with you at 10:30 on either of those days. When is good for you?"
Reply: "OK with me." (Click.)

I laughed when I heard this, as you may be doing, but the truth is that it's quite common, and in excess, there's nothing funny about it. The receiver of the message was either not listening or is not in the habit of communicating effectively via voice mail. Clearly her reply should've stated what day would be the most convenient.

Another problem arises when the person initiating the voice-mail communication leaves what I term a *metamessage*—a message about a message.

Message: "Got a quick question. Give me a call." (Click.)

Again, this is a widespread practice and an unnecessary waste of time—both the sender's and the receiver's. In this case, the sender should have stated the question so the receiver could have answered it in a return call or, if the answer was too lengthy, could have made some time to get together to go over it in person. The exchange then could've sounded something like this:

Message: "Got a quick question. Do you have the results of the survey we did for the XYZ Company?"

Reply: "Yes, got the results. I can send them over or we can make a time to meet. Let me know." (or "No, we don't have them yet, but we should be getting them by the end of the day on Friday. I'll call you as soon as they're in.")

The most important thing to remember is to keep voice messages as short and concise as possible. Thirty seconds should be your goal, but you should try not to go over a minute. This means planning in advance and using *SALES* to plan and organize.

A great voice-mail story from an investment bank client of mine concerns an industry publication that periodically recognizes financial analysts whose work it has identified as of a particularly high quality. It publishes their names, which are, in turn, seen by virtually everyone in the industry. These analysts gain tremendously from the publicity and are rewarded accordingly. A financial analyst for the investment bank attained this recognition without ever having spoken to reporters at the publication directly. All the communications between the two parties were accomplished via voice mail. It can be done.

Later in this chapter, under "Communicating via E-Mail and Voice Mail," I present a form that that will help you compose e-mails and voice mails that address various business issues. Several of these are adaptable to personal life. The form covers a lot of ground, so if you take some time to complete this exercise, you will have templates available the next time you have to send a similar message. Remember to use *SALES* as a tool to help you stay organized.

SPEAK(ER) TO ME

Boy, I hate it when people put me on speakerphone. Besides the fact that it is more difficult to hear, it makes me feel powerless and exposed. But if someone asks my permission first, then I feel just fine about it.

There are situations, now common, where using the speakerphone is a good idea. One is the ubiquitous conference call. Conference calls are planned in advance. They can have small groups of people on either end, can include people from several different locations, or be a very large virtual meeting. A typical example of the latter occurs when a public company announces financial results. There can be hundreds of people on a call, with analysts listening to the reporting by the upper management of the company such as the chief executive, chief financial officer, and perhaps a couple of other top managers. This is an occasion where technology is a double-edged sword; people used to have to gather for such an event. While not as many people would be present, managers would be able to use interpersonal communication to their advantage, and the presentation would be much more interactive. Today, the CEO or CFO will sit at company headquarters and report the results, reading from a prepared script to analysts in far-flung locales who have dialed in to a special number known as a *bridge line*. Let me tell you, this is mind-numbing stuff. There is usually a question and answer period at the end of the call, but by then everyone's senses have been fairly dulled. In fact, I think that these calls contributed to the stock market bubble burst and corporate malfeasance that regulators are still grappling with. Analysts, whose job it is to listen, can't help but tune out during these incredibly boring communications, missing vital information and not asking good questions. Technology giveth, and it taketh away.

Other types of conference calls are more effective in that they aren't so scripted, and real discussions take place. I've seen this done successfully repeatedly by my law firm clients, who frequently gather to discuss important matters with clients by telephone.

My favorite use of the speakerphone is when others join a one-on-one call. I have done this myself. I'll be speaking to a client, and an associate who needs to hear all or part of the conversation steps into my office. However, I don't just press the speakerphone button; I ask permission first: "Dave, Michael has just stopped in, and I think it would be good for him to hear what you have to say. I'd like to put you on speakerphone." I've never encountered a situation when the other party has said no.

Of course, if you want to display power and attempt to put another party at a disadvantage, then by all means put them on speakerphone without asking permission. This can be very effective during a tough negotiation or in an adversarial situation. Of course, when my friend's son recently placed me on speakerphone, he had the power thing all wrong.

The speakerphone is a great piece of technology if used correctly. So be cognizant of the following:

- The call becomes public, so anything you say will be heard (no putting your hand over the mouthpiece). If you must have a private moment, you must press the mute button and be sure it's working.
- There is a slight delay because the phone mechanism must sense the switch between speaking and listening. Overlapping speech can be lost or cause confusion. Be patient and wait for a second or two before speaking. (The advantages are that interrupting and shouting matches are fewer.)
- Vocal inflection is vital to the communication.

CLOSING THE LOOP

Today I received an acknowledgment to an RSVP to an invitation I had sent. This acknowledgment simply said, "Noted. Thank you." This is a very smart thing to do. It closes the loop on a communication. A serious flaw that has been exposed with our dependence on electronic communication has been the occasional but potentially disastrous lack of confirmation that a message has been received. I may send a message, but unless it is acknowledged, I cannot be sure that it has been received. Even if it is not returned to me as undeliverable, it may still have gotten lost in cyberspace.

This lesson was driven home to me a few years ago. I had promised a client information regarding some business we had been planning to do. I am very careful about keeping promises, so I e-mailed the information to her and waited for her to reply. It was a very busy time for me, and I lost track of the communication and let it get away from me. Two weeks later I realized I hadn't heard back from her, so I called her. She very apologetically told me that she had never received my e-mail, thought I wasn't interested, and had hired another company for the project. Naturally, I apologized profusely and told her that I had, in fact, sent the information as I had promised and was so sorry I hadn't followed up. That was a painful lesson. More recently, I did not receive a voice-mail message that was left for me. Not knowing to expect it, I could not be faulted for not receiving it. Just last week I received a message on Wednesday on my personal answering machine that I did not know was there until Saturday. The machine flashes if there are messages. Of course, I immediately accused each member of my family of listening to it without notifying me, even though they're a pretty reliable bunch. For some reason the message got buried. Fortunately, it wasn't anything earth shattering, but it scares me anyway. Closing the loop—confirming that messages have been received—is, in these times, an essential new piece of the communication protocol. A simple e-mail exchange regarding getting together with someone for lunch might look like this:

Ruth: "How about lunch Friday at 12 at the diner?"
Jane: "Sounds good, see you then."
Ruth: "Okay, see you Friday."

My final response closes the loop and assures Jane that I have gotten her RSVP. It's on both our calendars.

In short, the message cycle should look something like this:

- Sender sends message.
- Receiver replies to message.
- Sender acknowledges receiver's reply and closes loop.

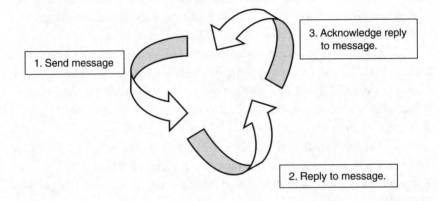

If you don't receive a response to a communication within a reasonable period of time, don't let it go. Call or e-mail again because it is quite possible that it got lost. And let's not forget about returning phone calls. It goes to the idea of being a reliable communicator. Make it a habit to return a call within 24 hours, 48 hours at the outside. It's also good manners to close the loop.

COMMUNICATING VIA E-MAIL AND VOICE MAIL

Write an e-mail and voice mail for each of the following:

1. *Schedule a meeting.*
   E-mail:

   _____

   _____

   _____

   _____

   _____

Voice mail:

_____

_____

_____

_____

_____

2. *Give the go-ahead for a project that was detailed last week.*
   E-mail:

_____

_____

_____

_____

   Voice mail:

_____

_____

_____

_____

3. *Follow up on information you sent.*
   E-mail:

_____

_____

_____

_____

   Voice mail:

_____

_____

_____

_____

4. *Follow up on information you asked for but did not receive.*
    E-mail:

    _____
    _____
    _____
    _____
    _____
    _____
    _____

        Voice mail:

    _____
    _____
    _____
    _____
    _____
    _____

5. *Follow up on information you received that was not what*
    you asked for.
    E-mail:

    _____
    _____
    _____
    _____
    _____
    _____

        Voice mail:

    _____
    _____
    _____
    _____
    _____
    _____

6. *Reply to the following message from a person senior to you: "I have a problem with the way you handled the chain of command. In the future, I want you to run these types of things by me first."*

E-mail:

_____

_____

_____

_____

_____

Voice mail:

_____

_____

_____

_____

_____

7. *Repeat number 6, but this time make it a person at your level instead of more senior.*

E-mail:

_____

_____

_____

_____

_____

Voice mail:

_____

_____

_____

_____

_____

8. *Deliver some news.*
    E-mail:

_____

_____

_____

_____

_____

    Voice mail:

_____

_____

_____

_____

9. *Give the results of a meeting.*
    E-mail:

_____

_____

_____

    Voice mail:

_____

_____

_____

_____

10. *Provide a status report.*
    E-mail:

_____

_____

_____

_____

Voice mail:

_____

_____

_____

_____

_____

E-mail and voice mail can be very effective forms of communication. Like all communication, however, they require some thought and planning. Our job as communicators is to see to it that these methods live up to their promise.

Ruth's Truths for Chapter 15

Ruth's truth 77: The ubiquity of e-mail has had a negative impact on people's interpersonal communication skills.

Ruth's truth 78: E-mail has become a way to avoid face-to-face communication.

Ruth's truth 79: E-mail and voice mail are the property of the company that owns the technology.

Ruth's truth 80: E-mails using proper grammar and spelling are easier to read and allow for quicker understanding.

Ruth's truth 81: Keep your emotions out of e-mail.

Ruth's truth 82: Avoid sending jokes and humor by e-mail.

Ruth's truth 83: Be aware of your tone.

Ruth's truth 84: Your outgoing voice-mail message is a public representation of you.

Ruth's truth 85: Make your outgoing message sound warm and friendly by using spoken rather than written language.

Ruth's truth 86: Incoming messages should be concise, organized, and replete with relevant information. They also should be short.

Ruth's truth 87: Take care when using a speakerphone.

Ruth's truth 88: Close the communication loop or risk getting lost in cyberspace.

Ruth's truth 89: Return calls within 24 to 48 hours, no longer.

Advance or Retreat: Determining When to Withdraw

There comes a time in everyone's life when efforts to communicate don't or no longer get the expected or desired results. For example, you cannot overcome objections every time you receive them. Some days are worse than others. People being people, they make mistakes, don't keep promises, trample the feelings of others, become angry, and generally transgress in all sorts of surprising and distasteful ways. This is as certain as the sunrise and completely unavoidable unless you never have human contact. As an old friend once told me when I was crying to her about my own hurt feelings, "Ruth, you get into relationships with people, they *do* things." This was simple but sage advice that I find comforting to this day. For some of us, these little disappointments can be the beginnings of real setbacks. Others seem able to take things more in stride and bounce back quickly.

There is considerable skill in being able to read and interpret signals, often nonverbal and thus subtle. This ability helps to guide reactions and responses. When it works, it governs our behavior, helping us to decide when to push and when to pull back. While pushing too hard is almost always a poor choice, doing it when being signaled to back off can be disastrous. Following are some ideas about how to deal with the inevitable reversals of fortune that we all must face.

REJECTION AFFECTION

How does being rejected make you feel? Are you fairly resilient and able to bounce back quickly from a rejection, or does it touch something deep within you and make you feel like a failure? Or do you have rejection affection? I've faced my share of rejection. I vividly remember rejections suffered when I was performing in New York, a business in which at least 80 percent of the professionals are out of work at any given time. Despite this fact, those rejections were among the most painful because of what they meant to me at the time: "No, sorry. You may not pursue your dream." During one period, while I was trying to get started as a jingle singer, a music producer criticized my voice, saying it didn't have the sound required for that type of work. It destroyed me to the extent that I did not make a single call or approach a single person in that business for six months. It was a good thing I had kept my day job. And looking back, what a colossal waste of time it was.

Another time I had taken a job as a sales rep for a music production company. The two owners paid me a commission on jingles I brought in, and I got to sing on all the jingles they produced. The caveat was that I had to sign over my residual payments to them, a considerable amount of money. Being very hungry at the time to amass jingles for a demo reel and not very confident about my abilities, I agreed. After a few months, I had sung on a number of successful national jingles, had collected enough samples for my reel, and decided to quit the job at the production company to pursue singing full time. The day I gave my notice, one of the owners of the company told me I should forget about pursuing jingle singing as a career. He told me it was never going to happen and that I was no _____ (a very prominent singer whom I considered a competitor). Oh, and he said that he was just telling me that for my own good; he didn't want me to get my hopes up and be disappointed. The next day I woke up with a nervous twitch in my eyelid. When I told my husband, an artist also familiar with rejection, about what had happened, he firmly said, "People are always going to say you can't, you're not good enough, find another line of work, and that they're only telling you for your own good. If you believe them, you give them power. If you go on and follow your dream, *you* have the power." He further pointed out that if I was so lousy, why did they use me on the jingles they were producing, and why did they sound so good that I would put them on my demo reel? I decided to take back the power I had so willingly given up. The twitch in my eyelid subsided. I completed paperwork that directed those residual payments back to me. (I later learned that it had been illegal for them to deprive me of that income in the first place.) As a result of that act, I had a good cushion of income and went out and plied my trade. I was working regularly within six months. It was a career that lasted 12 heady years. My voice was heard all over the world, and I made a lot of money doing something I loved. I cringe to think what could have happened if I had taken that owner's "advice." By the way, both he and the competitor are gone.

When I switched careers, I faced a whole new set of rejections. I was starting from scratch. No reputation, no colleagues, and no one I could turn to for mentoring or advice. I was alone and felt very isolated. But I had learned a great deal from my show business career. Most important, I learned that I could create something from nothing and gained tremendous confidence from that, which I can now communicate to others. As I've knocked on doors and had them slammed in my face, a critical skill I have learned is persistence. As I noted in Chapter 13, the more persistent you are, the more credibility you gain and the more people believe you've got something worth buying. By persisting, you create an image of stability that is highly valued.

Being able to manage rejection, to bounce back after each time it happens, is a signal that you believe in yourself. It is what I call *rejection affection*. It makes you stronger. This kind of self-confidence is very attractive to others. No matter what you do, rejection is part of life, and it is certainly and unavoidably a part of business. So, like stage fright, get used to it, and practice dealing with it. Remember to be discriminating about taking advice, accepting criticism, and dealing with rejection.

INTERPRETING SIGNALS

Clients and others have a variety of ways of communicating with us. Most direct is the verbal method:

- "You're doing a great job."
- "We're very happy with the work."
- "We'd like to discuss extending the contract."
- "We've decided to go with another supplier this year."
- "We won't be needing your services any longer."
- "We aren't interested in this product at this time."

I prefer direct communication. Direct communication is generally clear and, as a result, difficult to ignore or misinterpret.

With feedback or communication that is positive, many other signals are sent. Clients seem happy to see or hear from you, they agree to spend time with you, and they even invite you places and give you gifts. This is indirect communication. A good relationship, even if indirectly communicated, is fairly easy to discern. Unfortunately, negative or neutral feelings are much more difficult to figure out. Because they cause discomfort to both the sender and receiver, they tend to be avoided or are very vague. And receivers have a disturbing tendency to hear only what they want to hear. The combination of the two can cause serious problems. For example, sometimes these messages are surrounded by positive speech so that the real message is buried.

Claire, a client of mine, was having trouble with a temporary worker who had been hired to help out during a particularly busy time. The temp was spending time during the day surfing the Internet and not completing tasks he had been assigned. This was making Claire's job more difficult because she found herself finishing work that was supposed to have been done by the temp. She told me that although she had spoken to him, his work had not improved. So we did some role practice, and I asked Claire to pretend that I was the temp. Her demeanor and tone were serious. Following are the words she said:

> Don, do you have a minute? Great. First, I want to tell you you're doing a great job. There are a couple of areas, however, where we need to make some adjustments.

We were videotaping the session, and when I played it back, Claire was shocked to see just how ineffective she was. Because she didn't want to hurt his feelings, she sent a very mixed message that did not at all convey her real feelings. And Don heard what he wanted to hear, which was that he was doing a great job and therefore didn't have to make any changes.

Confusing or conflicting messages beg for clarification. When I get mixed messages, I try to paraphrase and get to the bottom of things:

> So I hear that while you're happy with the work I'm doing in general, there are a couple of things I need to do differently.

By paying attention to my own confusion, sensing that there is a mixed message, and asking the sender a clarifying question, I usually can get to the hidden message (see Chapter 10). In addition, I do the sender a favor by sparing him the burden of having to give me unpleasant news, and he is usually grateful for that.

In cases where the client is saying something negative directly, it is important to listen carefully with an open mind and respond:

> I'm sorry to hear that. As you might imagine, like you, we learn from getting feedback from customers, so it would be helpful to know why you've chosen to use someone else this time.

or

> I've been wanting to speak to you about _____ and have noticed that you don't seem as satisfied as before. Naturally, this concerns me greatly because it is always our intention to meet clients' needs. With that in mind, knowing whether there is a problem is the first step in improving delivery of this service [or product]. Can you tell me anything about that?

Because you are acting openly, it encourages the other communicator to respond openly, and the discussion actually may turn out to be quite fruitful.

The opposite also may happen: The client may not want to share the real story. The discomfort may be too great, or she may not want to hurt your feelings. There may well be other factors at work that she is embarrassed about or prevented from sharing with you. Perhaps she anticipates a tussle. Conflict avoidance is very common. If a client chooses not to share the true reasons for a change in the relationship, there's not much more you can do. However, here is one important consideration: *Don't read more into a rejection than it merits.* If you don't get the facts, don't automatically assume that the client doesn't like you or want to hear from you anymore. Even if a project goes badly, it doesn't mean that client will not give you another chance. Instead, do things that may be counterintuitive: Keep in touch periodically, let them know what you're up to, send interesting articles, and network in the same circles. Be persistent and exhibit stable, confident behavior even in the face of failure.

Do the following to help you interpret client signals:

- Be self-aware. If you are confused by a message, say so.
- Behave openly to encourage openness in others.
- Pay attention to nonverbal signals: vocal tone, facial expression, eye contact, and so on.
- Don't read too much into a client signal.

It is extremely difficult to peel away at clients' negative reactions and takes a high level of determination and skill. Still, it is not always possible to get answers. At those times it's important to have empathy. Nobody likes saying no, and yet some people have to do just that an awful lot. There is also a moment when you'll have to pull back, gather your strength, and move onto more positive ground.

DEALING WITH THE IRATE CLIENT

Clients, like other people, get angry and can become nasty and say gratuitous things. This is especially true when there is a great deal of money at stake. They may have paid for a product or service, and it isn't working out according to plan. This puts them in a difficult position in that not only do they have to answer to their superiors and clients, but they also have to tell the supplier who they feel is failing them. This type of pressure can lead to explosive behavior.

It's important to remember at these times that clients are people too. They respond to the same set of stimuli that other human beings do. When things aren't going well, there is a tendency to lash out, and they may not want to lash out at coworkers or direct reports because they have to face those people every day. And most people who value their jobs will avoid blasting the boss. Instead, they may choose to attack the most available person whom they determine to be free of risk to their careers. That person may just happen to be you. If a client does go on the attack, your best defense is to try to defuse the situation. To defuse, you have a couple of options:

- Remain silent until the client has finished, acknowledge the angry feelings, express regret or apologize, and see if you can move on from there:

  > I see you're upset about what has happened, and I'm very sorry about the way things turned out. I'd like to make amends. Can we spend some time discussing the situation so that we can come up with some ways to turn things around?

- If the client is using inappropriate or gratuitous language, attacking you personally, you do not need to tolerate it. Maintaining calm, you should tell the client gently but firmly that you hear how angry and upset she is, understand it, that you would like to make amends if possible, but would rather discuss it when tempers have cooled.

> I can see how angry and upset you are. I am very unhappy too and accept responsibility for the way things have turned out. I would like to discuss solutions to the problems, and I have some ideas about that, but I think it would be best to wait until tempers have cooled before we continue. When can we schedule some time?

Defusing highly charged situations puts them back on track so that a solution can be found. Maintaining a calm attitude in the face of such negativity is extremely difficult and requires intense self-control. However, it is the key to working through such situations. In addition, this may mean apologizing even if you don't think you've caused the problem.

THE FALLBACK POSITIONS: APOLOGIZING AND EXPLAINING

Speaking of apologizing or expressing regret, when is the last time you heard a politician or business executive say, "I did it, it was wrong, and I apologize." If a powerful, public person did come out and say those words, wouldn't it be refreshing? More important, wouldn't you like that person a little more, be more likely to forgive, and feel resentment diminish? The rhetorical art of apology has been neglected for too long. Communication scholars have been studying the rhetoric of *apologia* for decades and have found that it has reached its nadir in recent years. One reason for this is that litigation-phobic business executives and politicians have been persuaded by their advisors and attorneys that apologizing is akin to admitting wrongdoing, which can increase liability. But the decline of the rhetoric of apology as a conflict-management device has had a deleterious effect on our ability to generate trust and build relationships with others, the keys to success in life and work. In fact, this reluctance to admit wrongdoing and apologize for it has been shown to exacerbate bad situations and lead to full-blown scandals. Ignoring or glossing over mistakes, business or personal, complicates issues unnecessarily. It is time to rethink the ideas of apologizing and explaining and reintroduce this aspect of communication into our daily lives.

Apologizing and explaining are the perfect fallback position, an almost foolproof method of defusing an angry or unpleasant encounter of any kind.

They don't require a quick wit or good sense of humor, which means they're available to just about everyone. When things go awry, it is necessary to step back and alleviate the tension that has built up in such a situation. And get this, it works—and this point is critical—even if you did nothing wrong. Apology is an excellent tool for getting past the hard feelings and moving on.

Referring to mistakes and their aftermath, Deborah Borisoff and David Victor have found that "failure to acknowledge or to address a situation or occurrence can exacerbate difficulties between individuals."[1] A situation occurs where a conflict arises. Perhaps a mistake has been made, a deadline is not met, or a person's feelings are hurt. No one takes time to explain or apologize. The individual affected by these transgressions is left not only with the burden of a mess to clean up but also with the ill will generated by the hurt feelings and a deep feeling of mistrust that poisons the relationship and sets its future course on a negative path.

A client recently asked me to help her deal with an error she'd made at work. She had betrayed a confidence entrusted to her by her boss. It turns out that her boss had decided to seek a divorce, which was personal information that she had not told many others about yet. My client then told a colleague with whom she thought she had a good relationship, who was, she was surprised to find, hurt by the fact that the boss hadn't shared the same information with her. There was a level of competitiveness for the boss' attentions that my client had not properly assessed. The colleague divulged to the boss that she had found out about her separation, and although she did not name my client, the betrayed confidence was exposed. My client naturally felt guilty and bad that she had mishandled the situation. She also was somewhat resentful because she discovered the following day that another colleague also had the boss' personal tidbit and had been spreading it around. However, because that person and the boss were close personal friends, she was not suspected as the source of any leaks. My client didn't know what to do. I advised her to go to her boss, admit that the betrayal was hers (the boss' friend's indiscretion was irrelevant), explain why she did it to the best of her ability, and apologize. She said that there really was no excuse and that she was afraid of her boss' reaction. I told her that in this type of situation, the only thing she could do was to apologize, show herself as human and inclined toward occasional folly. However, it also would demonstrate her maturity in her being able to take responsibility for mistakes and courage in facing a difficult and unpleasant situation so directly.

The client bought my argument and approached her boss, who was gently reproachful but appreciative that she had confirmation as to where the breach had originated. At this moment my client said that she was very tempted to expose the so-called close friend of the boss but resisted, understanding correctly that it would have served no purpose and may even have alienated the boss further. The end result was that the boss let it slide, and their relationship grew. She also learned the value of carefully guarding confidences.

There is no communication device that works as well as apologizing and explaining when things go wrong. Colleges and universities have long included a section on their applications inviting students to explain any disciplinary actions. Along with some of the other communication skills, apologizing and explaining are so rarely undertaken that those who do it are viewed exceptionally positively. Rules for apologizing are

- Apologize as soon as possible after you become aware of a transgression. Sometimes we know immediately; in such a case, act immediately.
- Apologize if a client is upset and blaming you even if it is not your fault. In this type of situation you can try using the words "I regret" instead of "I apologize." The word *regret* is not as blameful.
- Accompany your apology with an explanation. Let the other party know that you understand what went wrong. This reassures that person that you have learned from the mistake and that it is unlikely to happen again.

The benefits of apologizing and explaining include

- They defuse conflicts.
- They demonstrate maturity and courage.
- They show sensitivity to others' feelings.
- They show a willingness to suspend your own ego.

SOOTHING THE PAIN

Having people angry with you is painful for most people; we aim to please and want to be liked. I was listening to a radio interview of former

Secretary of State Madeleine Albright, who was promoting her new autobiographical book. The interviewer noted that in the book Albright had said one of the most difficult aspects of her job as Secretary of State was its adversarial nature and the corresponding fact that so many people weren't going to or didn't like her. However, she knew that to be effective in her job, her discomfort with this reality had to be a secondary consideration, and she needed to find ways to get past it. She then laughed as she admitted that the deep desire she has to please others and make them like her is a problem that dogs her to this day. "I still want to be liked," she said during the interview. I thought this was a staggering admission from one of the world's most powerful people.

It's important to keep in mind that most mistakes and transgressions aren't personal attacks. If you can get around any tendency you might have to view them as such, these conflicts will be much easier to bear. A client who is a chief executive of a large company confessed to me that he becomes upset when someone nods off during a speech or presentation that he is delivering. He blames himself for being boring or not engaging everyone in the room. Now this executive is one of the most engaging and entertaining speakers I have ever seen. I suggested to him that perhaps the person who falls asleep was not bored at all but had not slept well the night before or for several nights. Maybe there was a new baby at home or a sick child who needed nighttime attention. In other words, it probably had nothing to do with my client's performance whatsoever. And anyway, he cannot control everyone in the room and should stop attributing every snore and bit of restlessness to his speaking ability.

Another tactic to keep yourself from getting beaten down by naysayers is to move onto the next possibility. Remember the saying "persistence persuades"? Well, being persistent ensures that you do not linger on negative outcomes. And there is something else to remember: A person can be persistent for years but spend too much time lingering on the rejections. Persistence, then, must be partnered with focusing on the positives, the successes. Concentrating on your goals will get the best payoff. My own experience of rejection in my first career as a performer that I talked about earlier in the chapter was a good example of how not to allow rejection to sidetrack aspirations.

However, good relationships built with care over time will go a long way toward mitigating the inevitable slipups. I have been surprised and delighted to see many of my own mistakes quickly forgiven by clients who have learned to rely on my ability to be forthright and direct. In fact, many of our relationships have grown much stronger as a result. This has been tremendously comforting and soothing and is perhaps the biggest benefit of confronting troubles head on.

WHEN WITHDRAWING IS THE CORRECT PATH

Occasionally, you have no choice but to withdraw. There are situations where the obstacles are so stacked against you that all the communication in the world cannot make a difference. These situations may require pulling up stakes and settling somewhere else. This could mean leaving a department or position, resigning a client, or parting ways with a friend. These decisions often are preceded by months of agonized consideration and are very personal. Once you decide that nothing more can be done, though, be confident in your assessment. There are many situations that an individual will find to be a good fit, but unless they are explored, they will go undiscovered.

Ruth's Truths for Chapter 16

Ruth's truth 90: Read nonverbal cues to know when to push and when to pull back.

Ruth's truth 91: Retain power instead of giving it to people who tell you that you cannot succeed.

Ruth's truth 92: Rejection may have nothing to do with the quality of your work, but even if it does, it may not mean the end of a relationship.

Ruth's truth 93: Be counterintuitive when facing a rejection by keeping in touch to show confidence, steadfastness, and resolve.

Ruth's truth 94: Deal with an irate client by working to defuse the situation.

Ruth's truth 95: Apologizing and explaining often defuse highly charged situations immediately.

Ruth's truth 96: Being forthright and direct encourages forgiveness.

Ruth's truth 97: Sometimes withdrawing is the correct path.

Some Final Thoughts

When I teach people about my passion for communication, one of my great fears is that they will go back to what they were doing the minute we have our final meeting. In fact, when I do one-day workshops, I always leave feeling a little down that I won't be there to continue to cheer them on and support them with my version of TLC—Tender Loving Criticism. I always invite people with whom I've worked to keep in touch, to follow up with me, or to contact me any time they would like a little shot in the arm of encouragement or a quick suggestion. Too few people take advantage of this, unfortunately. I think one reason is that they are mindful and respectful of my time, which I so appreciate even though I tell them it's included in the fee that has covered our scheduled work.

Yet, although clients often perceive this as generosity, this is not entirely true. In part, maintaining the connection with clients is not just for them but for me. I like knowing how they're doing and whether the skills they took from our work together are still functioning as they should. For example, if things have stopped working, it pays for us to explore why. Perhaps the client has grown beyond what she learned in a particular workshop or one-on-one coaching setting. Perhaps she's in a new position or new company with a completely new set of coworkers and rules and culture. Perhaps (and sometimes this does happen) she cannot use what I taught because I made some assumptions that weren't true. Whatever the reason, I need to know. It is therefore very important to continue evaluating and assessing, questioning, and exploring. Only by doing these things can you continue to grow as a communicator.

"AM I THERE YET?" A NEVER-ENDING PURSUIT

The great dancer and choreographer Martha Graham once said, "No artist is pleased. There is no satisfaction whatever at any time. There is only a queer, divine dissatisfaction; a blessed unrest that keeps us marching and makes us more alive than the others."

The process of becoming a better communicator, of *Get Them to See It Your Way, Right Away* described in this book, is one that is lifelong. Even with mastery, there is always more to be done. People are often shocked when I tell them that I never stop auditing my skills, trying to improve them, because I know that I can always be better. I often tell friends and clients that I'm just not happy unless I'm unhappy—that "divine dissatisfaction," perhaps. One big negative in having this type of disposition is that my family finds me frustrating. They have to live with someone who is not easily satisfied with her own substantial accomplishments. They often translate this to mean that I am not satisfied with them. And I am difficult. I expect them, especially my children, to do their best, and sometimes I ask too much of them. They and all of us frequently need to sit back, relax, and take stock, to give ourselves a pat on the back for a job well done and to reward ourselves appropriately.

I understand why people want to feel as if they're finished, however. The process of becoming a better communicator is so arduous and painstaking that it's a relief to imagine that someday it will be over. So I can only say, "Sorry, but it doesn't end here." In fact, if you are reading this book, you're either working on and within the process or beginning it. Wherever you are in the process, though, there is always more to do. Remember those gifted communicators I talked about at the very beginning of this book? They are always—*always*—working on improving their skills, just as a gifted musician always must practice. Mozart, a musical genius, practiced until his fingers bled. Because we live in such a changeable world, we must be adapting and adjusting our style constantly.

So what's next?

- Take every opportunity to build your skills.
  - Take classes.
  - Read everything you can get your hands on.

- Ask colleagues for feedback.
- Hire a personal coach.
- Get more formal education (college or graduate).
- Practice every chance you get.
  - Network as much as you can.
  - Go to business social events.
  - Take a leadership position in a professional association. (This may be one of the best avenues to learning to *Get Them to See It Your Way, Right Away!*)
  - Go to industry conferences and conventions.
  - Practice on your friends.
- Acknowledge and reward yourself for jobs well done
  - Take a day off.
  - Treat yourself to a massage or similar self-care service.
  - Take a long weekend and stay in an inn or hotel where you can be pampered.
- Develop an interest in other people.
  - Draw them out by asking questions and probing for information.
  - Listen empathetically and respond accordingly.
  - Volunteer for or join the board of a non-profit organization.
- Learn to accept criticism as a venue to improve in your work or personal life—not as a personal attack.
  - Learn to deliver criticism in a tender, loving, constructive (TLC) way.
  - Learn to say you're sorry.

PRACTICING AND PREACHING

Books like this one may purport to have all the answers, but the truth is that the world is a big place with many people, all of whom are different. Different people have unique styles, inhabit different environments, and thus require different approaches to communicating. Therefore, while all the techniques written about here are sound, if they don't work for you, *throw them out, and try something else!* I love preaching about the benefits and value of good communication and practice all the things I've discussed, but I don't always succeed. Sometimes I have to regroup. As I mentioned in the preceding section, I want to hear from you about the things that work and those that don't. Send me your stories and experiences so that I can continue to learn.

Getting people to see it your way by communicating well is deep and complicated. But if it is done well, it is incredibly rewarding. Selling oneself or one's products and services sincerely, thoughtfully, and creatively is not phony, slick, or manipulative. It is, as I hope I have demonstrated, painstaking and full of bumps in the road. Impressions are formed very quickly that influence communication outcomes. The better the outcome, though, the more able you will be to further a culture of communication, encouraging others to extend themselves in similar ways. This book has laid out some important steps to take on what is a lifetime journey filled with unique and exciting situations that require often complex and nuanced responses. Take these steps, however, and you are well on your way to building the confidence and appeal that will identify you as a player, someone who not only has the expertise necessary to get the job done but one who, in the process, also provides an enlightening and enjoyable ride for all involved. Someone who can *get them to see it your way, right away!*

Ruth's Truths for Chapter 17

Ruth's truth 98: The pursuit of communication mastery is never-ending.

Ruth's truth 99: If the strategies in this book don't work for you, throw them out, and try something else.

Ruth's truth 100: Rules are meant to be broken.

Notes

CHAPTER 1

1. *Webster's II New Riverside University Dictionary* (Boston: Riverside Publishing Company, a division of Houghton Mifflin, 1984), p. 1060.
2. *Ibid.*

CHAPTER 3

1. DiResta, Diane. *Knockout Presentations: How to Deliver Your Message with Power, Punch and Pizzazz* (Worcester, MA: Chandler House Press, 1998).

CHAPTER 4

1. Goleman, Daniel. *Working with Emotional Intelligence* (New York: Bantam Books, 1998).
2. *Ibid.*
3. *Ibid.*

CHAPTER 5

1. See Chapter 6 for detailed information about the communication location.
2. Mitchell, Jack. *Hug Your Customers: The Proven Way to Personalize Sales and Achieve Astounding Results* (New York: Hyperion, 2003).

CHAPTER 6

1. Your home should be clean, neat, and organized. It is not important for it to be beautifully or expensively decorated.

CHAPTER 7

1. PowerPoint information technology has become obligatory in many situations. And while I love graphics, there are almost always too many slides and ones that are very poorly prepared. I urge my clients to fight against the current fad and exclude PowerPoint or similar programs. A couple of strategically selected graphs or charts on paper would serve the same purpose and would eliminate the barrier to communication.

CHAPTER 8

1. Tannen, Deborah. *Talking from 9 to5: How Women's and Men's Conversational Styles Affect Who Gets Heard, Who Gets Credit and What Gets Done at Work* (New York: William Morrow, 1994).

CHAPTER 9

1. RoAne, Susan. *What Do I Say Next? Talking Your Way to Business and Social Success* (New York: Warner Books, 1997).
2. Burley-Allen, Madelyn. *Listening: The Forgotten Skill* (New York: Wiley, 1995).

CHAPTER 10

1. Many experts define *closed questions* as requiring a yes or no answer.

CHAPTER 11

1. Goldin-Meadow, Susan. *Hearing Gesture: How Our Hands Help Us Think* (Cambridge, MA: Harvard University Press, 2003).

CHAPTER 12

1. Mitchell, Jack. *Hug Your Customers: The Proven Way to Personalize Sales and Achieve Astounding Results* (New York: Hyperion, 2003).

CHAPTER 15

1. The desktop computer is also a place where it pays to be cautious; if you are, for instance, looking for a job, it is best not to write your cover letters on your office computer. Whether or not they are saved only on your desktop and not on the company server, they are the property of your company. Even if you delete them from the desktop, they are, amazingly enough, not really gone and, therefore, still can be retrieved. So be very careful.
2. How we process information we receive through the ear versus how we process information we receive through the eye differs. Think of how differently we use language when we speak as opposed

to when we write. We use contractions, we stop and start, we use vocal and physical expression. Writing is mostly verbal; meaning is derived from the word itself. Speaking is mostly nonverbal; meaning is derived from how we look and sound.

CHAPTER 16

1. Borisoff, Deborah, and David Victor. *Conflict Management: A Communication Skills Approach* (Englewood Cliffs, NJ: Prentice-Hall, 1989).

Ruth's Truths

Ruth's truth 1: The simple act of reaching out to people and trying to connect is an act of persuasion.

Ruth's truth 2: Selling and pitching should be honest, genuine, and born of a deep interest in other people.

Ruth's truth 3: People who are adept at selling and winning over others seek first to give in order to receive by doing more than they have been asked to do.

Ruth's truth 4: A sound selling relationship is marked by a mutual satisfaction of needs.

Ruth's truth 5: To be successful at winning over others, y'gotta like people.

Ruth's truth 6: Becoming a good communicator takes careful and systematic practice.

Ruth's truth 7: People form impressions about others within seconds of meeting or speaking with them, and these initial impressions are hard to change.

Ruth's truth 8: Leaving a good impression takes planning.

Ruth's truth 9: Set goals to give yourself the best chance of getting what you want out of life.

Ruth's truth 10: Write down goals and plans for achieving them.

Ruth's truth 11: Revisit and revise as needed.

Ruth's truth 12: Set smaller goals as incremental steps to larger ones.

Ruth's truth 13: The most important traits of charismatic people do not cost money to acquire.

Ruth's truth 14: Preparation is the single most important and single most neglected communication skill.

Ruth's truth 15: Take *A.I.M.* Thoroughly analyze and plan before entering the situation.

Ruth's truth 16: IQ is less important in business than emotional intelligence.

Ruth's truth 17: Relationships are the foundation of self-promotion.

Ruth's truth 18: Build relationships with people at all levels of the organization.

Ruth's truth 19: Self-disclosure is a catalyst to building relationships.

Ruth's truth 20: You must be able to regularly articulate and promote accomplishments; otherwise, people won't know what you've been up to.

Ruth's truth 21: Put yourself in others' shoes before attempting to criticize or give feedback.

Ruth's truth 22: Learn as much as possible before embarking on a communication.

Ruth's truth 23: The Internet is a good source of surface information.

Ruth's truth 24: Remote communication is a good adjunct but not a substitute for direct communication.

Ruth's truth 25: It is the job of the supplier of services or products to uncover client needs.

INTERVIEW *Ruth's truth 26:* To get to the heart of a client's needs, ask the question, "What would you like to be different . . . ?"

Ruth's truth 27: Sometimes you have to assess client needs on the spot, so be prepared for this possibility.

Ruth's truth 28: Whenever possible, important communication should be conducted on your own turf, whether it be your office, home, or another location of your choosing.

Ruth's truth 29: Meals are excellent venues for doing business.

Ruth's truth 30: Dinner parties are good ways to demonstrate organizational skills and build business relationships.

Ruth's truth 31: Breakfast is a little used but effective business meal.

Ruth's truth 32: When meeting on foreign turf, try to explore it first; directly is best, but remotely is fine if there is no other practical choice.

Ruth's truth 33: Seize opportunities to communicate that occur every day.

Ruth's truth 34: Develop an introductory pitch that concisely tells what you do and what's in it for the listener.

Ruth's truth 35: Practice delivering your introductory pitch.

Ruth's truth 36: Determine your main message.

Ruth's truth 37: Define your objective.

Ruth's truth 38: Organize your thoughts by using *SALES*.

Ruth's truth 39: Use stories to give life to data and information.

Ruth's truth 40: Personal stories are best.

Ruth's truth 41: Transitions and segues facilitate communication by connecting different sections, forming a cohesive unit.

Ruth's truth 42: Notes, used effectively, help to keep you focused and on track, adding to the impression of poise and confidence.

Ruth's truth 43: Small talk facilitates the move into "big talk."

Ruth's truth 44: Conversational rituals are the basis for small talk.

Ruth's truth 45: Read as much as possible, but especially large newspapers.

Ruth's truth 46: Clip articles and keep them in a file to which you can refer.

Ruth's truth 47: Listening is critical to success and very rarely done well.

Ruth's truth 48: Good listeners are hard to find.

Ruth's truth 49: Listening is relaxing, fun, and very interesting.

Ruth's truth 50: Strive for level 1, intent listening in important personal relationships and in business.

Ruth's truth 51: Questions are the seeds of conversation.

Ruth's truth 52: Open questions elicit more information than closed questions.

Ruth's truth 53: Questions control the conversation.

Ruth's truth 54: Seek agreement through advance selling.

Ruth's truth 55: Objections are opportunities to ask questions and uncover hidden needs.

Ruth's truth 56: Anticipate objections and prepare answers.

Ruth's truth 57: You must make an emotional connection to communicate successfully.

Ruth's truth 58: Emotions are communicated nonverbally.

Ruth's truth 59: Nonverbal communication helps you to think.

Ruth's truth 60: To be believable, the verbal and nonverbal messages must be consistent with and not contradict each other.

Ruth's truth 61: Do a nonverbal self-assessment.

Ruth's truth 62: Read the room. Nonverbal communication must be attuned to the audience.

Ruth's truth 63: Lack of preparation to communicate is a cardinal sin.

Ruth's truth 64: Stage fright goes with the territory.

Ruth's truth 65: Practice is the antidote to stage fright.

Ruth's truth 66: Countless opportunities are lost because of lack of follow-up.

Ruth's truth 67: Have the courage to face people when delivering bad news.

Ruth's truth 68: Use a PDA and contact management software to keep track of follow-up activities.

Ruth's truth 69: Write personal, handwritten thank-you notes on unique cards and use a nice stamp.

Ruth's truth 70: There is a fine line between following up and pestering. Read the situation, and don't be a pest.

Ruth's truth 71: Not only is it important to like people, but it's also important to be liked.

Ruth's truth 72: Impeccable manners will make you a standout.

Ruth's truth 73: Regulate how you use your cell phone.

Ruth's truth 74: Be polite.

Ruth's truth 75: Keep promises.

Ruth's truth 76: Maintain confidences.

Ruth's truth 77: The ubiquity of e-mail has had a negative impact on people's interpersonal communication skills.

Ruth's truth 78: E-mail has become a way to avoid face-to-face communication.

Ruth's truth 79: E-mail and voice mail are the property of the company that owns the technology.

Ruth's truth 80: E-mails using proper grammar and spelling are easier to read and allow for quicker understanding.

Ruth's truth 81: Keep your emotions out of e-mail.

Ruth's truth 82: Avoid sending jokes and humor by e-mail.

Ruth's truth 83: Be aware of your tone.

Ruth's truth 84: Your outgoing voice-mail message is a public representation of you.

Ruth's truth 85: Make your outgoing message sound warm and friendly by using spoken rather than written language.

Ruth's truth 86: Incoming messages should be concise, organized, and replete with relevant information. They also should be short.

Ruth's truth 87: Take care when using a speakerphone.

Ruth's truth 88: Close the communication loop or risk getting lost in cyberspace.

Ruth's truth 89: Return calls within 24 to 48 hours, no longer.

Ruth's truth 90: Read nonverbal cues to know when to push and when to pull back.

Ruth's truth 91: Retain power instead of giving it to people who tell you that you cannot succeed.

Ruth's truth 92: Rejection may have nothing to do with the quality of your work, but even if it does, it may not mean the end of a relationship.

Ruth's truth 93: Be counterintuitive when facing a rejection by keeping in touch to show confidence, steadfastness, and resolve.

Ruth's truth 94: Deal with an irate client by working to defuse the situation.

Ruth's truth 95: Apologizing and explaining often defuse highly charged situations immediately.

Ruth's truth 96: Being forthright and direct encourages forgiveness.

Ruth's truth 97: Sometimes withdrawing is the correct path.

Ruth's truth 98: The pursuit of communication mastery is never-ending.

Ruth's truth 99: If the strategies in this book don't work for you, throw them out, and try something else.

Ruth's truth 100: Rules are meant to be broken.

Index

About the Author

Ruth Sherman is an internationally respected authority on speech and interpersonal communication and the president of Ruth Sherman Associates, L.L.C., an executive consulting and training firm.